# MY GIANT
## SEEK AND FIND
# ACTIVITY
# BOOK

priddy ☺ books
big ideas for little people

# Find it

Circle the objects that match the description below each box.

## green sock

## yellow fruit

# Hidden picture

Look at the farm scene. Can you find the objects pictured below?
Check the boxes when you find them.

# How to draw

Learn how to draw a dinosaur in three easy steps.

**1**

Draw a
half circle.

**2**

Give your dinosaur
legs and back plates.

**3**

Finish it with
a face, spikes,
and scales!

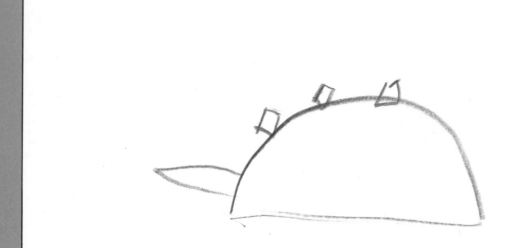

# Find the detail

Draw a line from the pictures to where they are in the house.

# Odd one out

One of these circles is different from the rest. Can you find it?

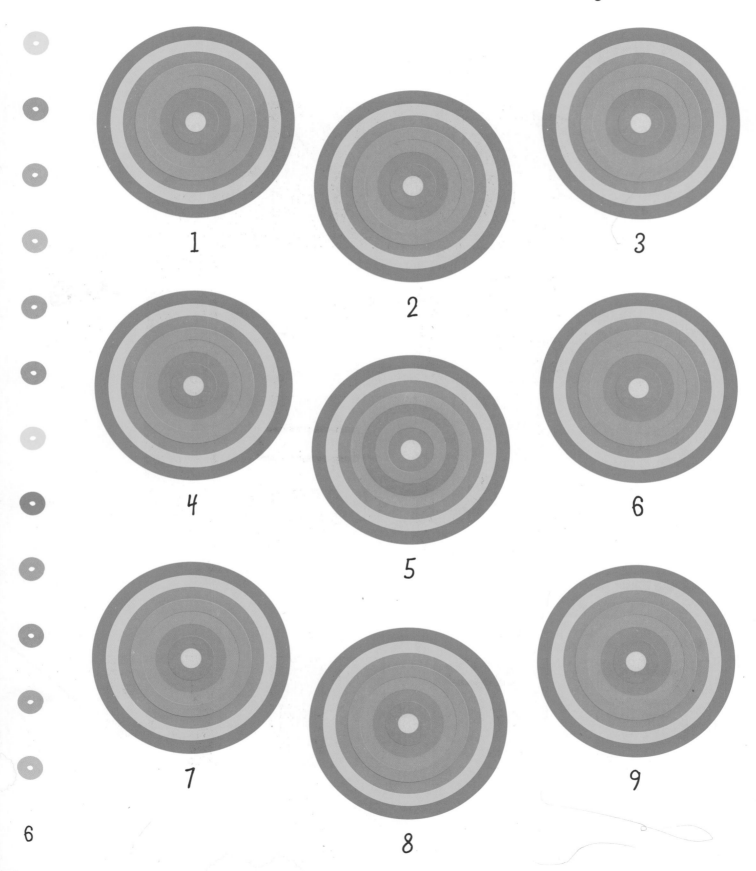

1

2

3

4

5

6

7

8

9

# Spot the difference

There are five differences between the two family pictures.
Circle them when you find them.

# Color me in

Color in this yard scene, using the colored dots as a guide.

# Word puzzle

Use the word and picture clues to figure out what the four mixed-up words are. Write the letters in the correct spaces.

A red flower

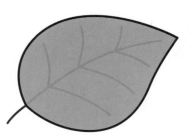

On a tree

A slimy bug

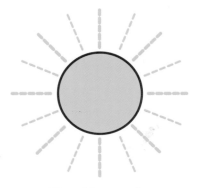

In the sky

r _e o s_

s e o

l _ _ _ _

e f a

s _ _ _ _ _ _

n i a l

s _ _ _

n u

# Color and create

Draw and color an African safari scene. Look at the pictures on the right for ideas, and add the things you like!

Can you draw trees like these?

You could add a very tall giraffe.

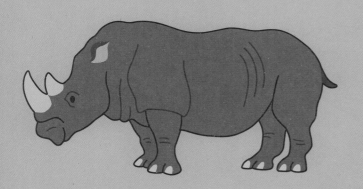

Why not draw a rhinoceros?
Is he friendly or fierce?

How about an African elephant?

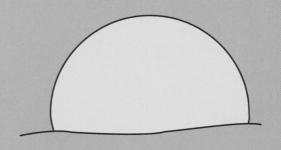

Don't forget to give the zebra
a black-and-white-striped mane.

Add a yellow sun or red sunset
to make the scene come alive.

# Jigsaw jumble

Which jigsaw piece completes the picture of the bowl of strawberries? Can you draw it in?

a

b

c

12

# Coloring fun

How many of these hobbies do you like?

# Copy it

Can you draw a drum? Draw it. Copy it. Color it in!

Look at the picture.

Draw over the outline.

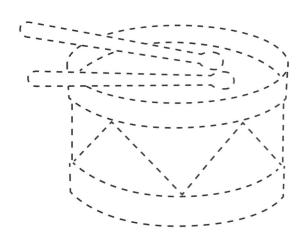

Now draw your own drum and color it in.

# Hidden picture

Look at this construction site. Can you find the objects pictured below? Check the boxes when you find them.

# Coloring fun

Make this picture out of this world!

# Match it

Draw lines to match the three pairs of gloves.

Draw lines to match the food with the flag.

Japan

Italy

United
Kingdom

Fish and
chips

Sushi

Pizza

# Picture sequences

Color in the last picture in each row to finish the pattern.

# Seek and find

The toys below are all hidden in the picture.
Check the boxes when you find them.

☐    ☐    ☐    ☐    ☐    ☐

# Copy it

Can you draw a teddy bear? Draw it. Copy it. Color it in!

Look at the picture.

Draw over the outline.

Now draw your own teddy bear and color it in.

# Word search

Can you find the farm words in the word search?

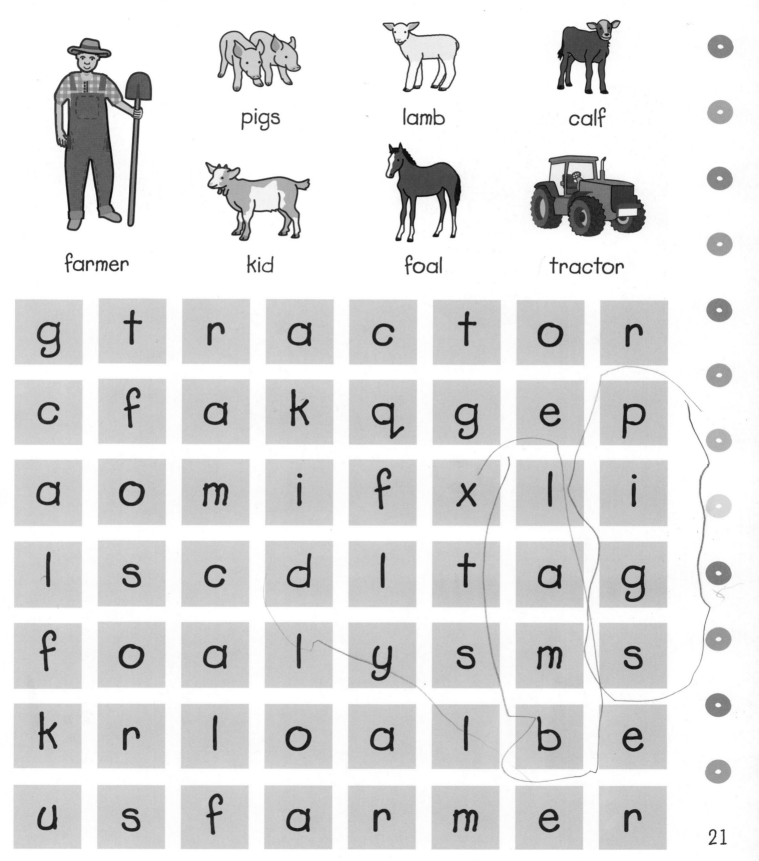

pigs

lamb

calf

farmer

kid

foal

tractor

| g | t | r | a | c | t | o | r |
|---|---|---|---|---|---|---|---|
| c | f | a | k | q | g | e | p |
| a | o | m | i | f | x | l | i |
| l | s | c | d | l | t | a | g |
| f | o | a | l | y | s | m | s |
| k | r | l | o | a | l | b | e |
| u | s | f | a | r | m | e | r |

# What's wrong?

Circle three things that don't belong in this yard scene.

# Outer space

This space picture contains lots of different shapes.
Can you spot them all? Check the boxes when you find them.

triangle ☐    circle ☐

square ☐

star ☐    rectangle ☐

# Big and small

Small, big, bigger, biggest! Can you sort these trees into size order, starting with the smallest?

What about these sandwiches? Which one would you eat?

# Hidden picture

Look at the pirate ship. Can you find the objects pictured below?
Check the boxes when you find them.

# Body match

Draw lines from each word to the correct place on the picture.

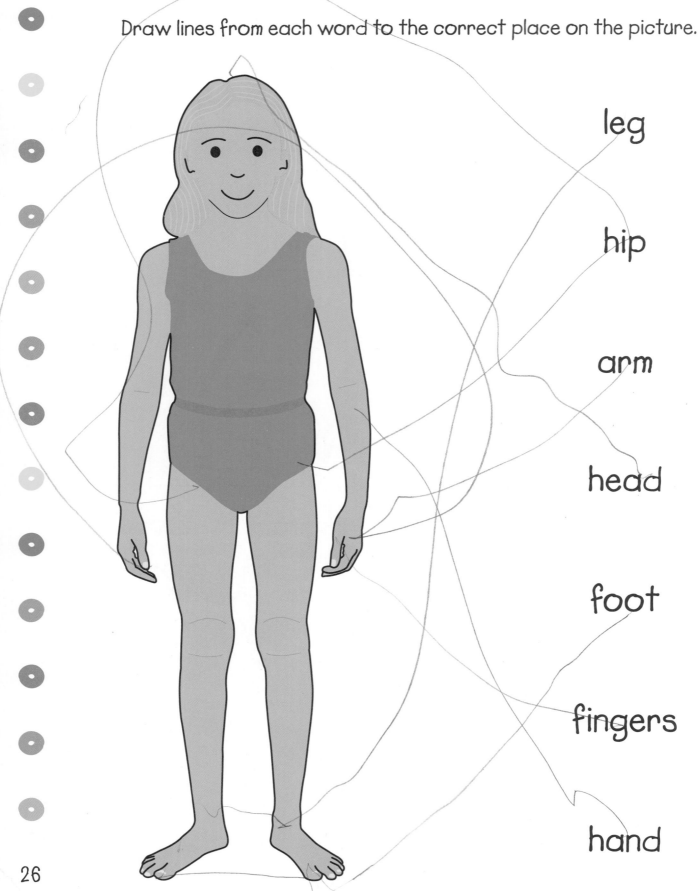

leg

hip

arm

head

foot

fingers

hand

26

# Dot-to-dot

Connect the dots to draw the submarine.
Color in the ocean scene to complete your picture.

# Word wheel

Fill in the missing letters of the shape words. Use these letters to spell the name of the shape at the bottom of the page.

Square

Triangle

circle

heart

_ _ _ _ _

# Color match

Write over the color words, and then draw a line
to where they are on the rainbow.

yellow     green

purple     red

blue     orange

pink

# What color am I?

Draw a line to match the color with the object.

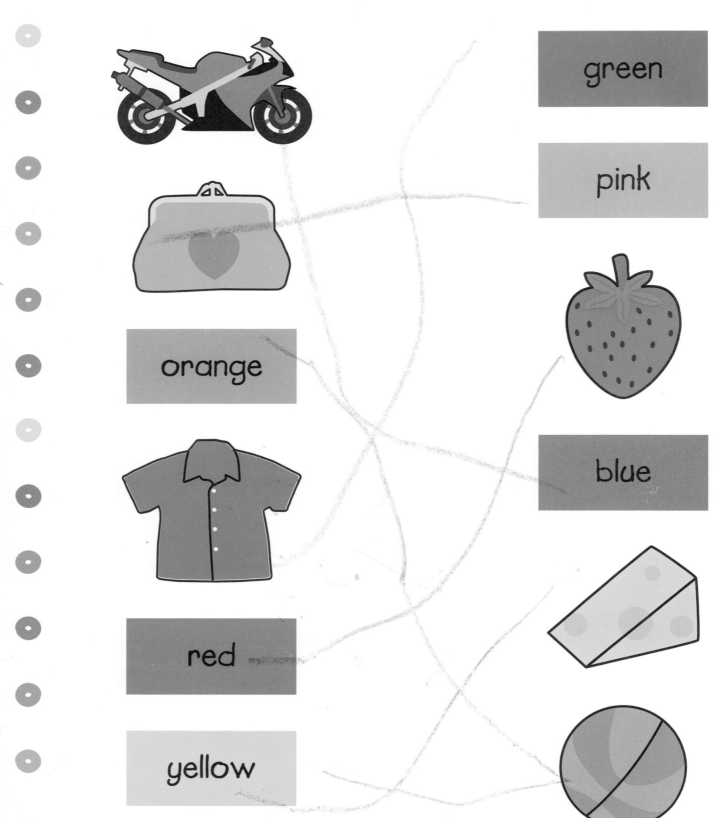

green

pink

orange

blue

red

yellow

# Missing halves

Can you draw the missing halves of these soccer pictures?

jersey

pitch

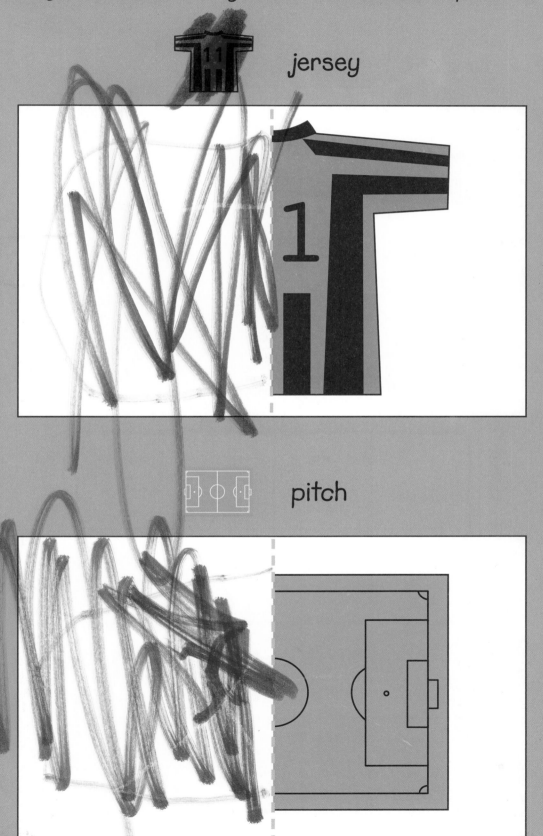

# Number sudoku

Fill in the numbers 1, 2, 3, or 4 into the empty squares. Each number must appear once in each row, column, and box of four squares.

Look at this example:

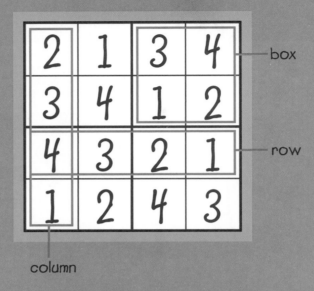

box

row

column

Now try these sudoku puzzles.

| | 2 | | 1 |
|---|---|---|---|
| 3 | | 2 | 4 |
| 1 | 3 | | 2 |
| 2 | | 1 | 3 |

| 1 |   | 3 | 2 |
|---|---|---|---|
| 3 | 2 |   |   |
| 4 |   | 2 |   |
|   | 3 | 4 | 1 |

| 4 | 1 |   | 3 |
|---|---|---|---|
|   | 2 | 4 |   |
|   |   | 3 | 2 |
|   | 3 |   | 4 |

# How many flowers?

Circle the T-shirt with five flowers.

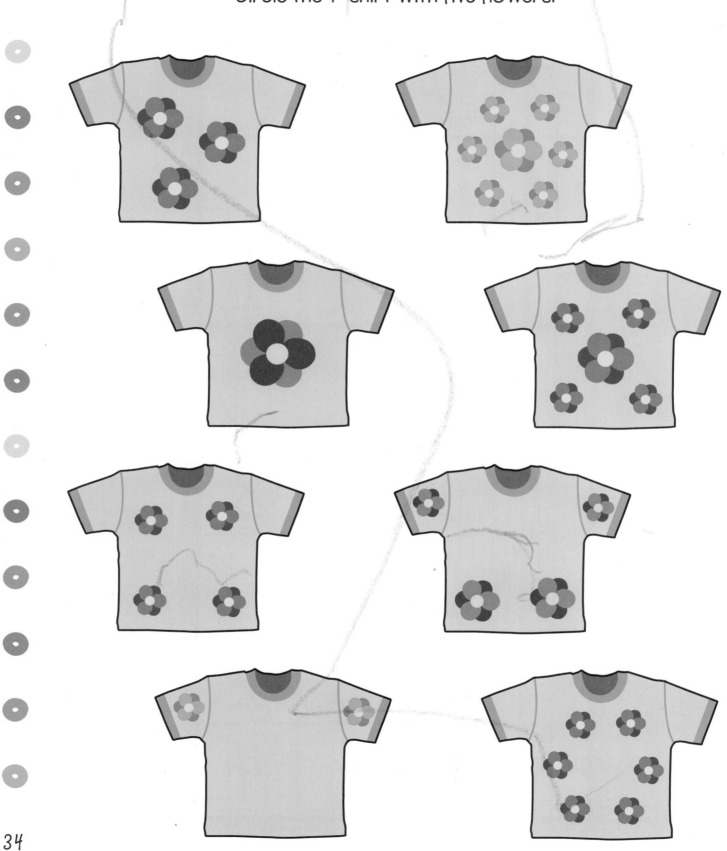

# Find and count

Can you find and count the items below?
Check the boxes as you find them.

1 cozy bed ☐

2 mirrors ☐

3 strawberries ☐

4 lamps ☐

5 blue chairs ☐

6 clocks ☐

7 apples ☐

8 pink socks ☐

# Farm foods

Write over the names of the foods we get from the farm.

eggs    cereal

cheese    milk

# Mouse maze

Find a way along the purple lines to lead the mouse to the cheese.

# Find and count

Can you find and count the food items below?
Check the boxes as you find them.

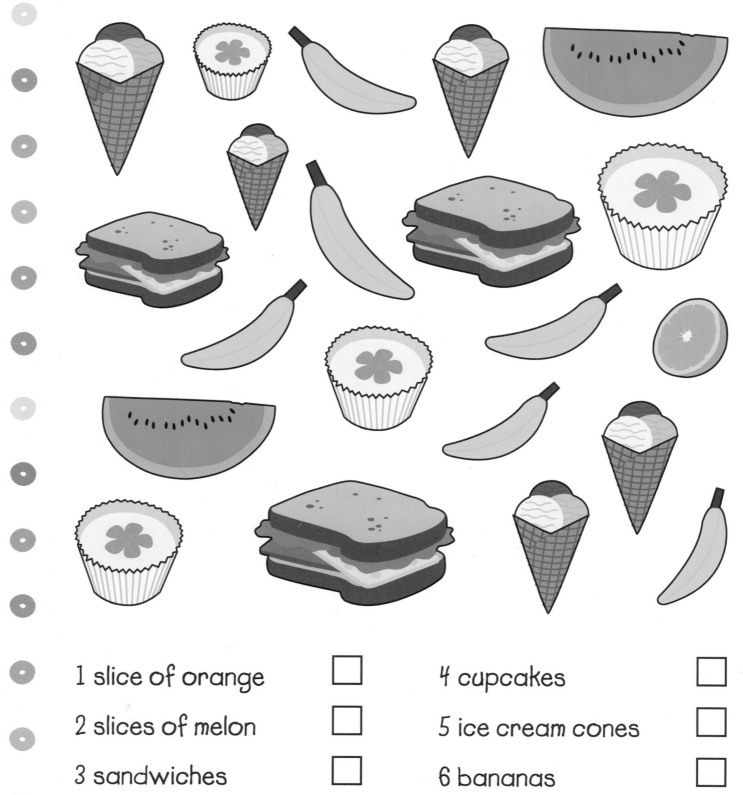

1 slice of orange ☐     4 cupcakes ☐

2 slices of melon ☐     5 ice cream cones ☐

3 sandwiches ☐     6 bananas ☐

# Hidden picture

Look at this coral reef scene. Can you find the objects pictured below? Check the boxes when you find them.

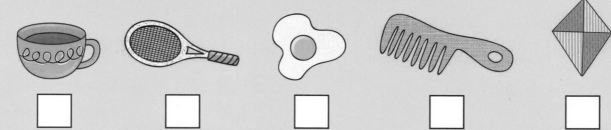

# Shape sudoku

Fill in the grids so that each shape appears once
in each row, column, and box of four squares.

Look at this example:

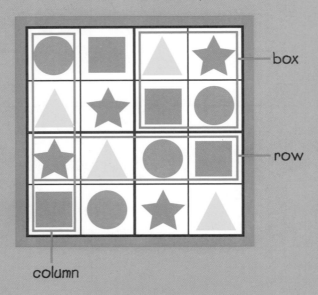

box

row

column

Now try these sudoku puzzles.

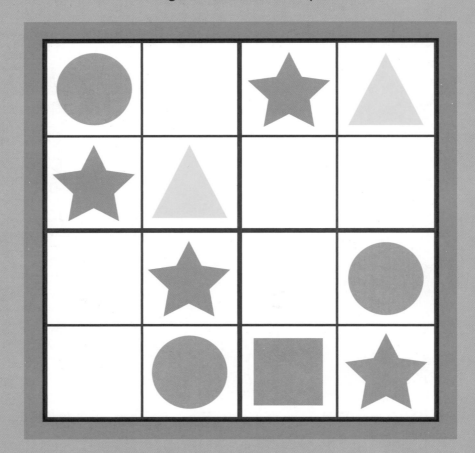

40

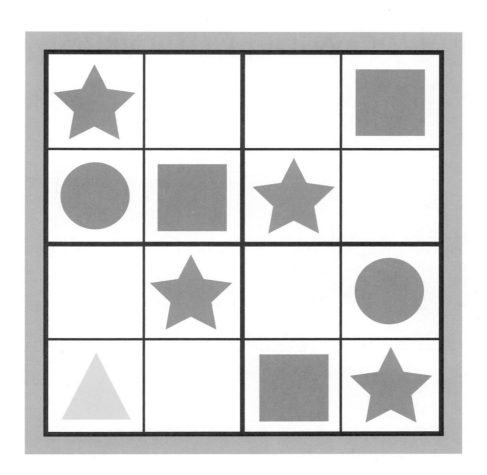

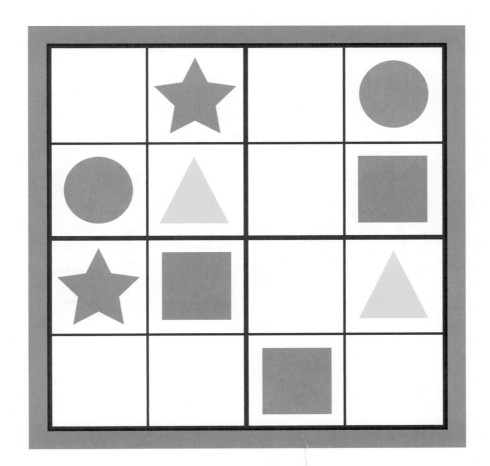

41

# Drawing numbers

Follow the instructions to complete the number pictures.

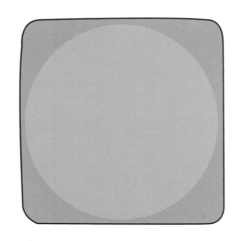

Draw two wheels
on the car.

Add five spots
to the dice.

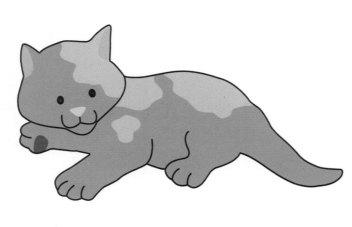

Draw six whiskers
on the kitten.

Add three more flowers
to the bunch.

# Crossword

Use the picture clues to help you complete the wild animal crossword.

1. giraffe

2. lion

3. monkey

4. panda

5. elephant

6. leopard

# Coloring fun

Color in this busy construction site.

44

# Spot the difference

There are five differences between the two prehistoric pictures.
Circle them when you find them.

# Follow the trails

Which trail leads the race car driver to his car?

# How to draw

Learn how to draw a dolphin in three easy steps.

**1** Draw half
a circle for
the body.

**2** Give your dolphin fins
and a bottlenose.

**3** Add extra detail
and a dot for
an eye!

# Hidden picture

Look at the space scene. Can you find the objects pictured below?
Check the boxes when you find them.

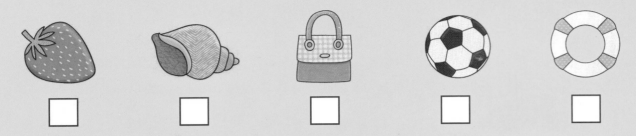

48

# I spy...

Can you find the animal that begins with each letter?

p

c

k

d

f

t

m

r

# Coloring fun

It's time to get out your princess-colored pens!

# Matching numbers

Count each group of objects, write over the numbers,
and match the two together!

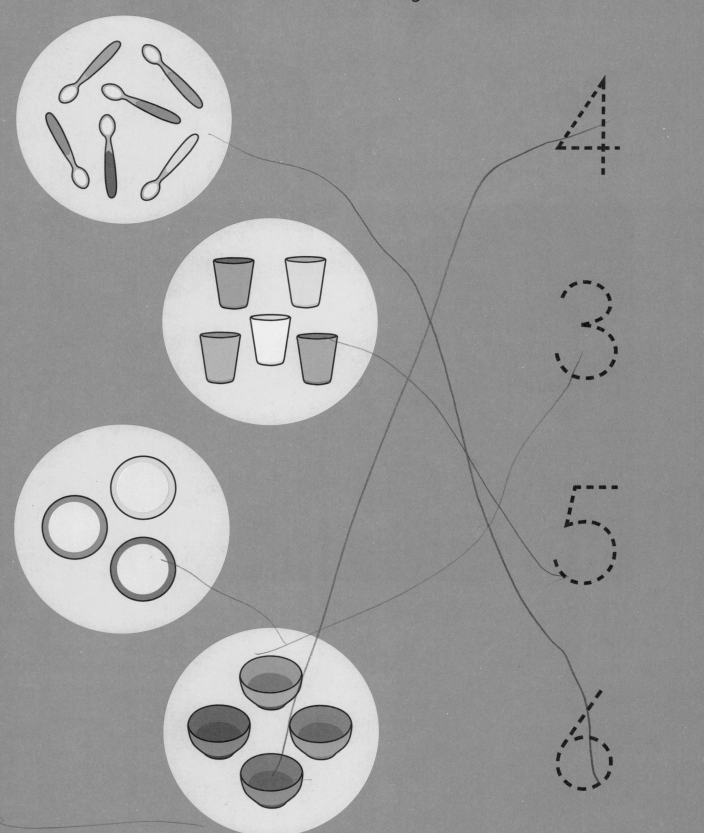

# Find and count

Can you find and count the items below?
Check the boxes as you find them.

1 swing ☐

2 boots ☐

3 cats ☐

4 watering cans ☐

5 birds ☐

6 red flowers ☐

7 worms ☐

8 butterflies ☐

# Pets at home

Count the pets, and then write the totals in the boxes.

goldfish

rabbits

guinea pigs

puppies

turtles

mice

# Coloring fun

Here are some cute pets. What colors will you make them?

# How to draw

Learn how to draw a boat in three easy steps.

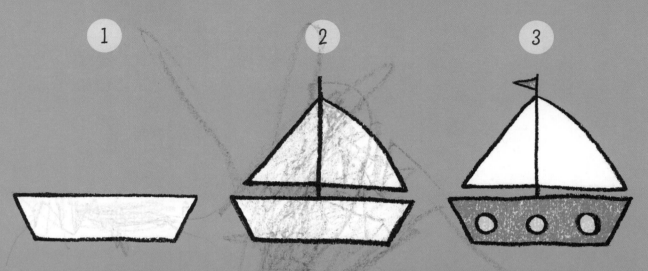

1. Draw the hull.

2. Draw two triangles for sails.

3. Add flags and portholes!

# Matching noises

Draw a line between each farm animal and the noise it makes.

baa baa

quack

oink

cock-a-doodle-doo

moo

naa naa

# Hidden picture

Look at this zoo scene. Can you find the objects pictured below?
Check the boxes when you find them.

    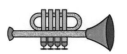

# Shape match

Draw a line between each object and the shape it matches.

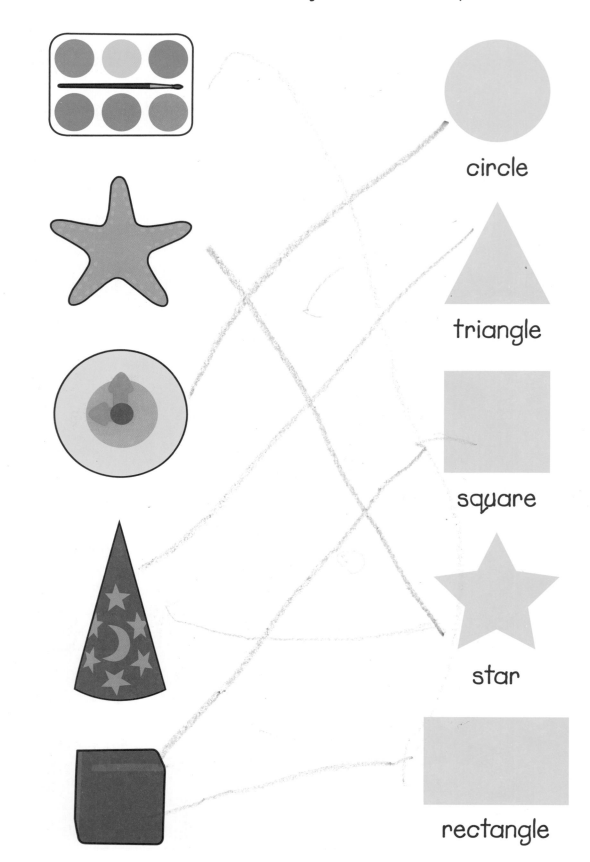

circle

triangle

square

star

rectangle

# Coloring fun

Give this seaside scene a splash of color!

# Number sudoku

Fill in the numbers 1, 2, 3, or 4 into the empty squares. Each number must appear once in each row, column, and box of four squares.

Look at the example:

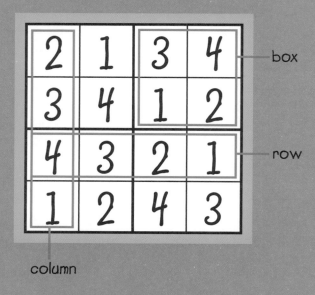

box

row

column

Now try these sudoku puzzles.

| 2 |   |   | 4 |
|---|---|---|---|
| 1 | 4 | 2 |   |
|   | 1 |   | 2 |
|   | 2 | 3 |   |

| 4 |   |   | 2 |
|---|---|---|---|
| 2 | 3 |   | 4 |
| 3 |   | 2 | 1 |
|   | 2 |   |   |

|   |   |   | 2 |
|---|---|---|---|
|   | 4 | 3 |   |
| 4 | 2 |   | 3 |
| 1 |   |   | 4 |

# Jigsaw jumble

Which jigsaw piece completes the picture of the koala?
Can you draw it in?

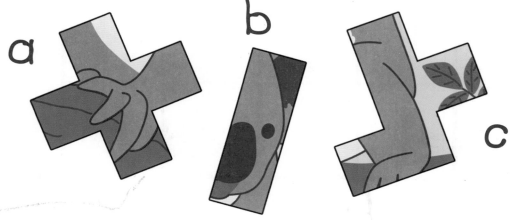

a

b

c

# Follow the trails

Which trail leads Misty the dog to her puppy?

# Hidden picture

Look at this store scene. Can you find the objects pictured below?
Check the boxes when you find them.

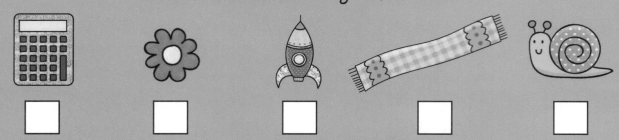

# In the ocean

Draw over the dotted lines, and then color everything in.

# Spot the difference

There are six differences between the two kitten pictures.
Circle them when you find them.

66

# How to draw

Learn how to draw a frog in three easy steps.

**1**

Draw a body.

**2**

Draw the eyes
and legs.

**3**

Finish with the feet
and a froggy face.

67

# Animal patterns

Look at the animals' markings,
and then circle the patterns that match them.

 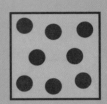

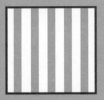 

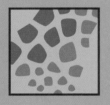 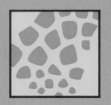

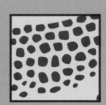 

68

# Coloring fun

What color are all these things? You choose.

# Matching pairs

Can you match the farmyard moms with their babies?
Draw a line between each animal pair.

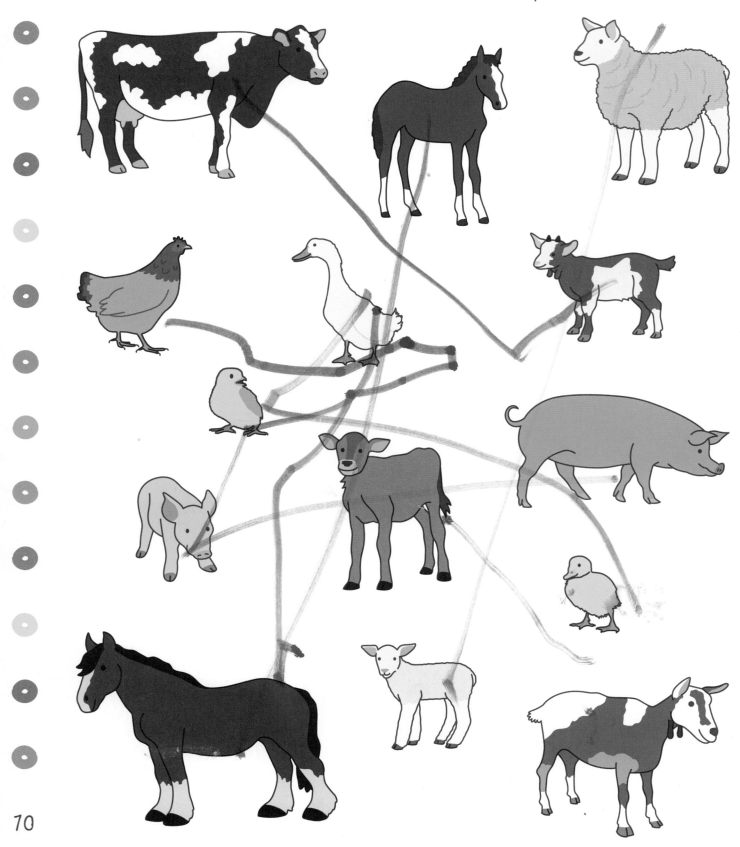

# Find it

Circle the objects that match the description below each box.

purple flower

blue car

# Hidden picture

Look at this playground scene. Can you find the objects pictured below? Check the boxes when you find them.

# Follow the trails

Which trail leads Farmer Joe to his tractor?

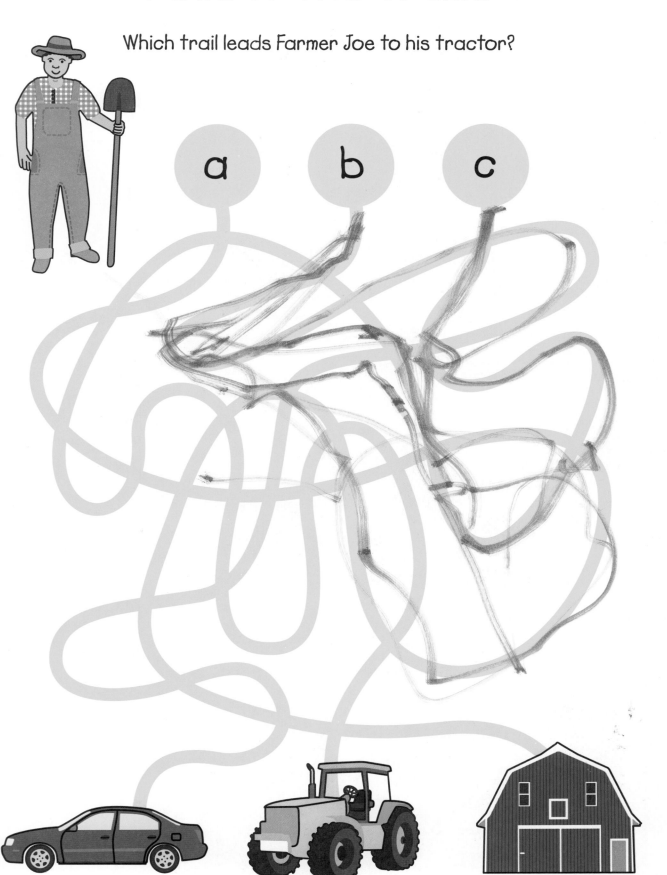

# Counting questions

Answer the questions below, writing your answers in the boxes.

How many yellow things can you count?

How many things are not green?

How many things are the wrong color?

# In the jungle

Write these words in the correct spaces underneath each animal.

frog    tiger    toucan    snake    gorilla

# Letter search

Can you find six things in this sea-life scene that begin with the letter "s"? Check the boxes when you find them.

seagull ☑    shell ☑

seahorse ☐    starfish ☐

shark ☑    sun ☐

# Animal habitats

Use the word and picture clues to figure out what the four mixed-up words are. Write the letters in the correct spaces.

I live in the desert.

c _ _ _ _ _

m e l a

I am from Africa.

z _ _ _ _ _

a e b r

I live in the ocean.

w _ _ _ _ _

h e l a

I am from Australia.

e _ _ _

m u

# Big and small

Small, big, bigger, biggest! Can you sort these animals into size order, starting with the smallest?

a

d

b

c

What about these wild animals?

a

b

c

d

# How to draw

Learn how to draw a car in three easy steps.

**1**

Draw a
rectangle and
add two wheels.

**2**

Draw
the roof.

**3**

Finish your car
with two windows.

# Blastoff!

Draw over the dotted lines, and then color in the rocket scene.

# Shapes fun

Count the number of sides each shape has, draw over the numbers, and then draw a line to the shape they match.

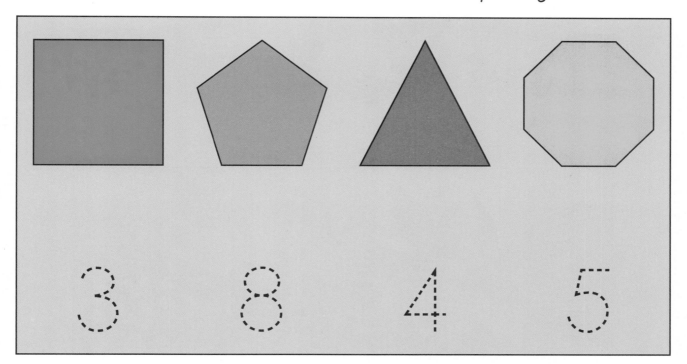

3    8    4    5

# On the rock

Circle the bug that has eight legs.

# Seek and find

The animals below are all in the picture.
Check the boxes when you find them.

☐ ☐ ☐ ☐ ☐ ☐

# Color and create

Bring this motorcycle picture to life by adding details and color.

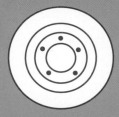

Make sure you finish the wheels.

Add some smoke behind to make it look as if it's going fast!

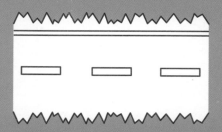

Draw the road and any other details you like.

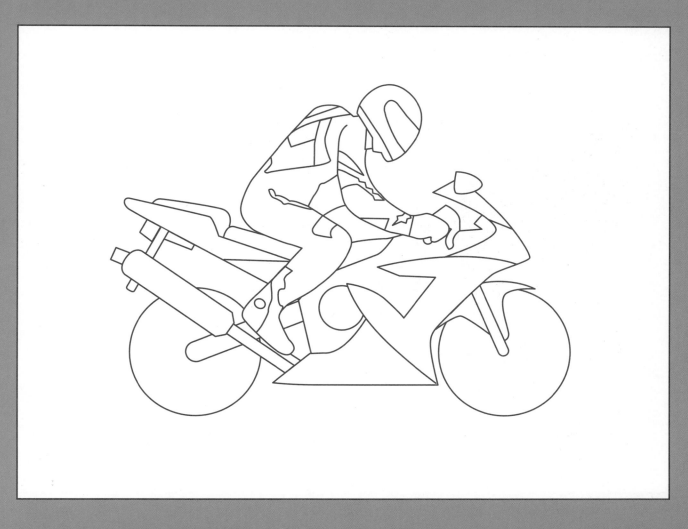

# Animal facts

Look at these animal groups. Can you answer the questions?

## At the poles

Which polar animal has wings? Circle your answer.

## Farm babies

Which farm baby has a coat made of wool?
Circle your answer.

# Number puzzles

How many stars can you see in the sky? Circle your answer.

8    10

7    9

How many arms does this starfish have? Circle your answer.

3    6

4    5

How many horns does Triceratops have? Circle your answer.

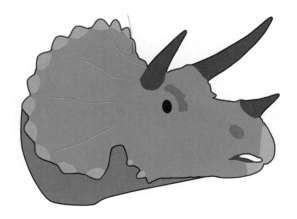

3    6

4    5

85

# Missing letters

Using the four letters below, can you complete each word?

# c o l c

_hair    du__k

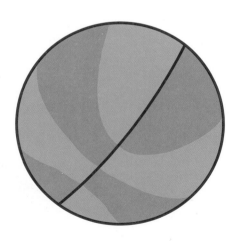

bo__k    bal__

# Hidden picture

Look at this cowboy camp. Can you find the objects pictured below?
Check the boxes when you find them.

# Dot-to-dot

Finish the house by connecting the dots, and then color it in.
Don't forget to make the sun shine.

# Number sequences

Write the number on the last jersey to complete the number pattern.

| | | | |
|---|---|---|---|
| 1 | 2 | 3 | 4 |
| 2 | 4 | 6 | |
| 6 | 5 | 4 | |
| 1 | 2 | 4 | |
| 10 | 8 | 6 | |

# Colorful flags

Color in the big flags, using the little flags as a color guide.

South Africa

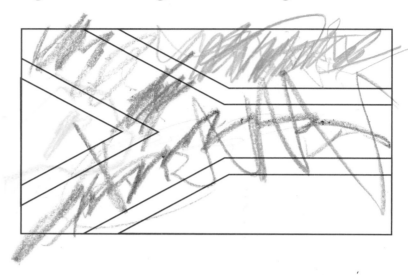

United Kingdom

Australia

# Coloring fun

Finish this picture of fabulous flying machines, and color it in.

# Space maze

Follow the white lines to find a way through the maze
to help the space shuttle land on the planet.

# Word search

Can you find the bug words in the word search?

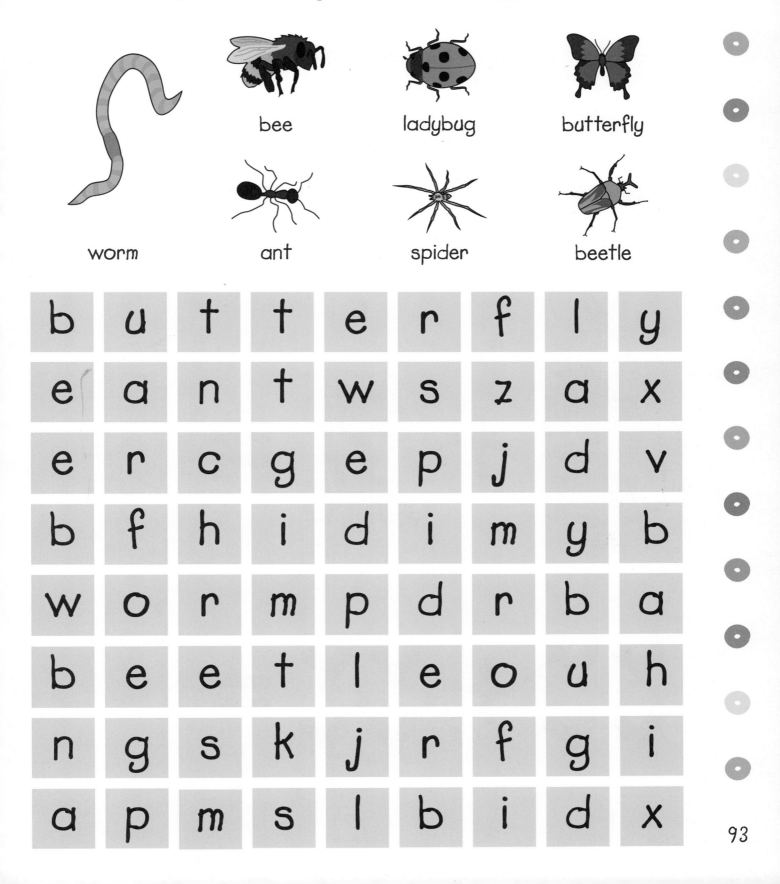

bee  ladybug  butterfly

worm  ant  spider  beetle

| b | u | t | t | e | r | f | l | y |
|---|---|---|---|---|---|---|---|---|
| e | a | n | t | w | s | z | a | x |
| e | r | c | g | e | p | j | d | v |
| b | f | h | i | d | i | m | y | b |
| w | o | r | m | p | d | r | b | a |
| b | e | e | t | l | e | o | u | h |
| n | g | s | k | j | r | f | g | i |
| a | p | m | s | l | b | i | d | x |

# Farmyard math

Add the first group to the second group,
and then write the totals in the box.

**+** means "add together"

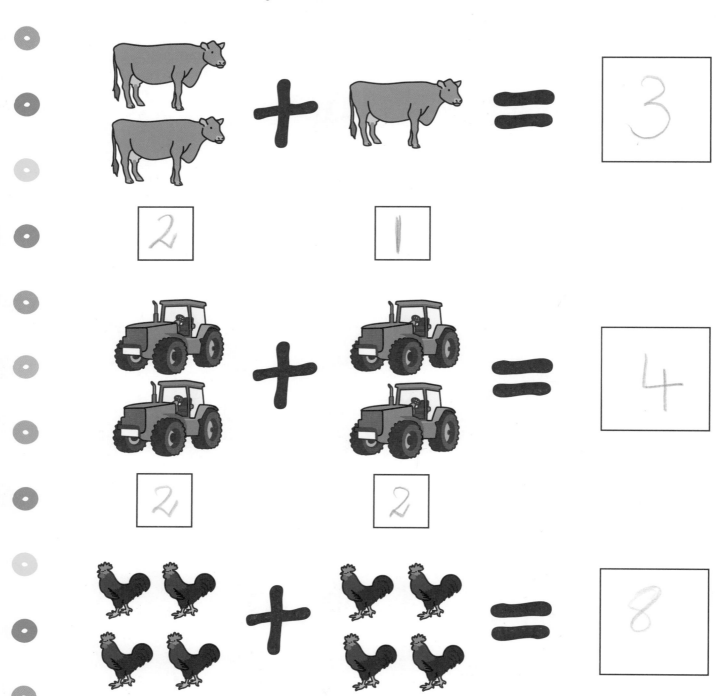

# In Africa

Which group has the most giraffes? Circle your answer.

How many zebras can you see on the African plain?
Write your answer in this box.

4

# Crossword

Use the picture clues to help you complete the space crossword.

1. moon

2. sun

3. astronaut

4. stars

5. planet

6. rocket

# Hidden picture

Look at this fairy scene. Can you find the objects pictured below?
Check the boxes when you find them.

 ☐  ☐  ☐  ☐  ☐

# Shape sudoku

Fill in the grids so that each shape appears once
in each row, column, and box of four squares.

Look at the example:

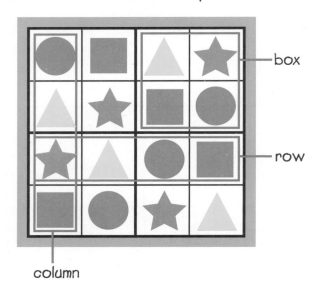

box

row

column

Now try these sudoku puzzles.

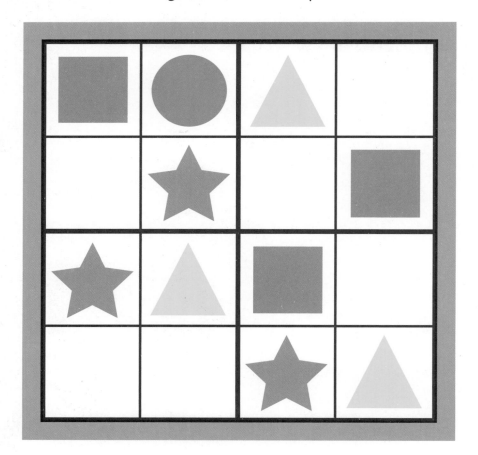

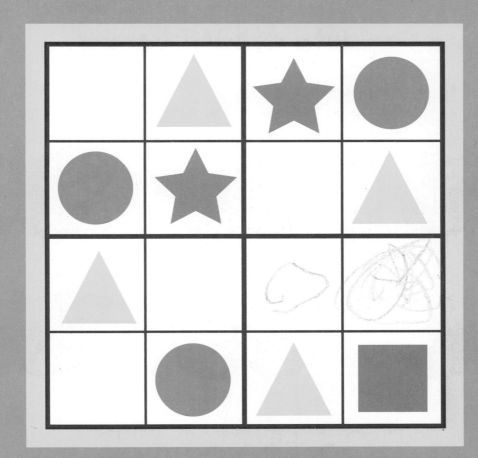

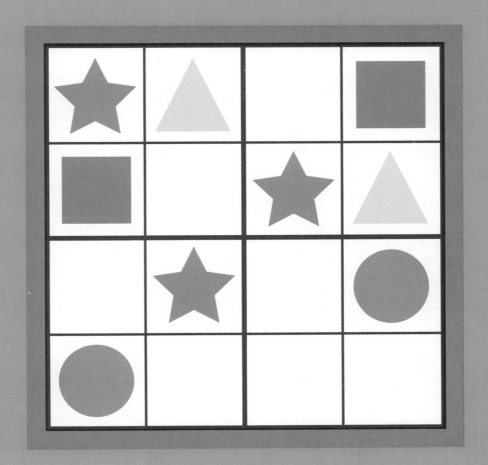

# Busy bugs

Two of the butterflies are exactly the same. Circle which ones.

# On the road

Which two fire trucks are exactly the same?

# What's wrong?

Circle four things that are wrong with this beach scene.

# Domino puzzle

Draw the correct number of dots on the blank dominos,
matching the ones beside them. The first one has been done for you.

# Colorful flags

Color in the big flags, using the little flags as a color guide.

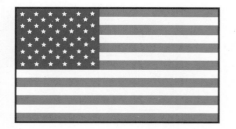

## United States of America

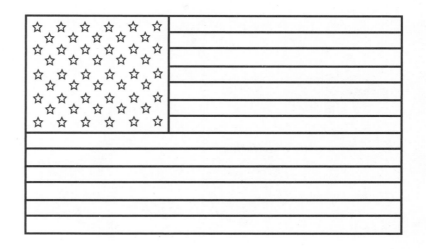

## Wales

## Brazil

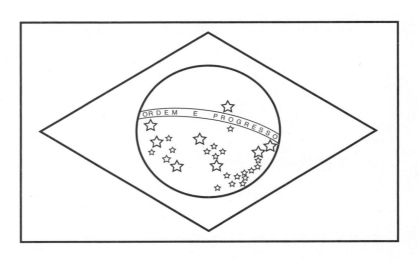

# In space

Count the space things, and then write the totals in the boxes.

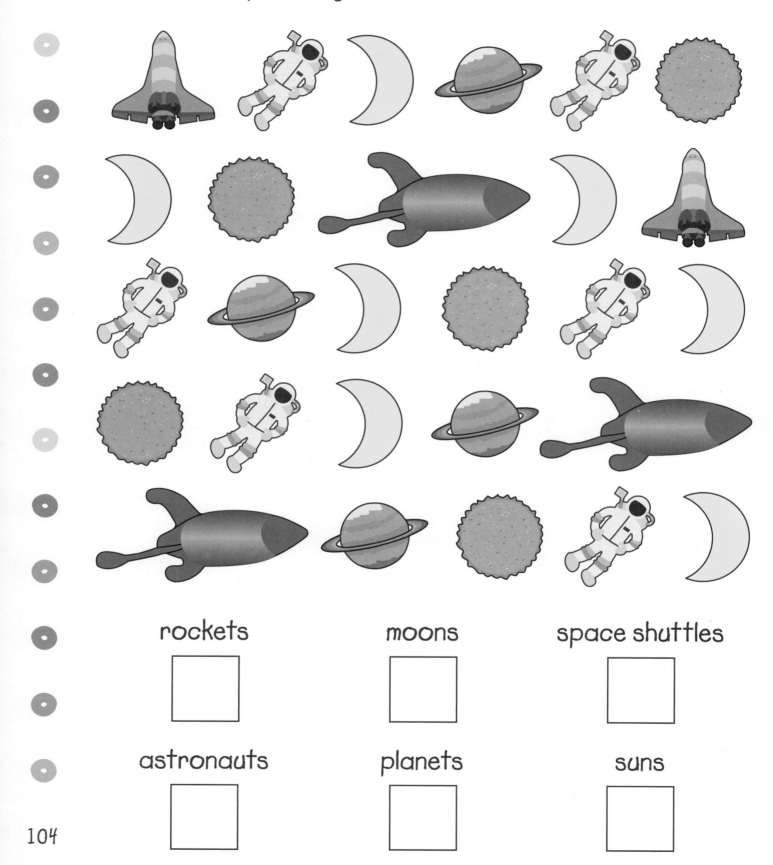

rockets

moons

space shuttles

astronauts

planets

suns

# Missing halves

Can you draw the missing halves of these vehicle pictures?

car

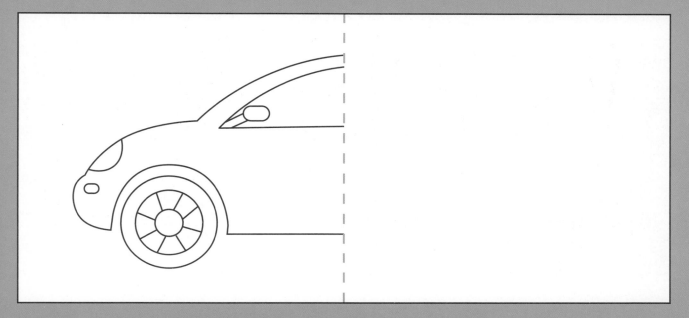

fire truck

# How to draw

Learn how to draw a butterfly in three easy steps.

**1**     **2**     **3**

Draw a
small body.

Add a wing
on both sides.

Give your butterfly a
face and antennae.

# Hidden picture

Look at the farmyard scene. Can you find the objects pictured below?
Check the boxes when you find them.

☐ ☐ ☐ ☐ ☐

# Shape sudoku

Fill in the grids so that each shape appears once
in each row, column, and box of four squares.

Look at the example:

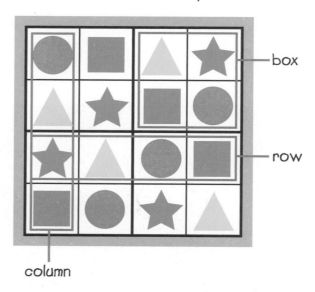

box

row

column

Now try these sudoku puzzles.

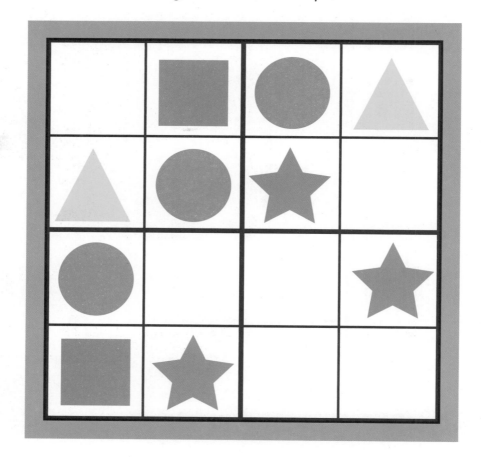

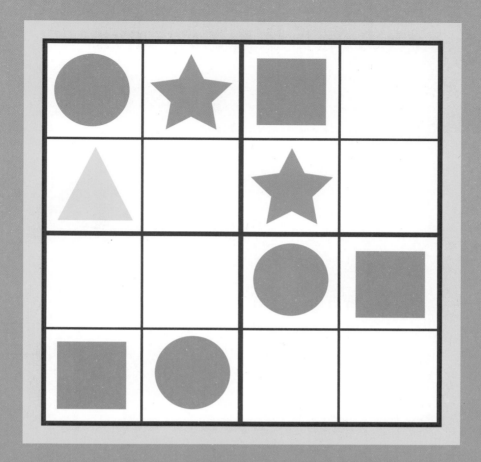

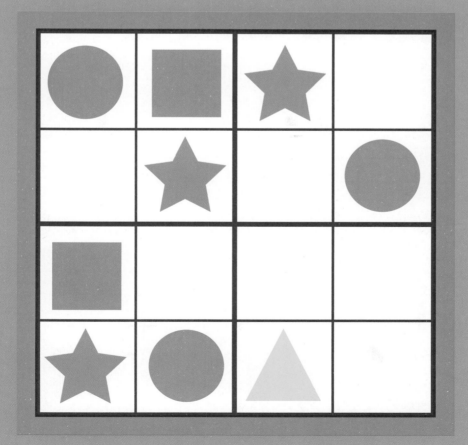

# Coloring fun

What color are all these farm animals? You decide.

# Yard search

Can you find the things below in this yard scene?
Check the boxes when you find them. Which one isn't there?

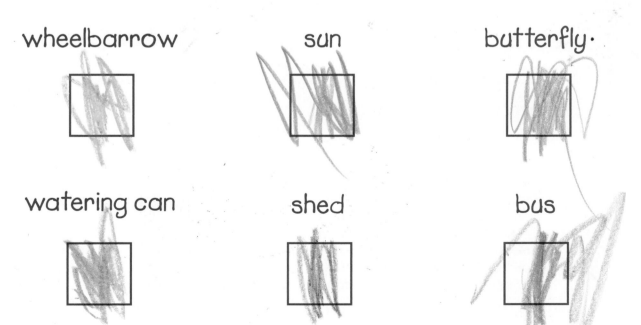

wheelbarrow

sun

butterfly·

watering can

shed

bus

# Color match

Circle the flags that include only the colors red, white, and blue.

Australia

France

Germany

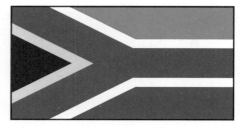

South Africa

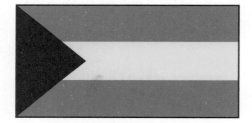

Bahamas

Chile

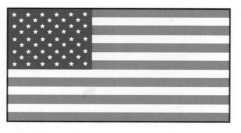

United States of America

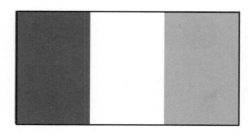

Ireland

# Jigsaw jumble

Which jigsaw piece completes the picture of Egypt?
Can you draw it in?

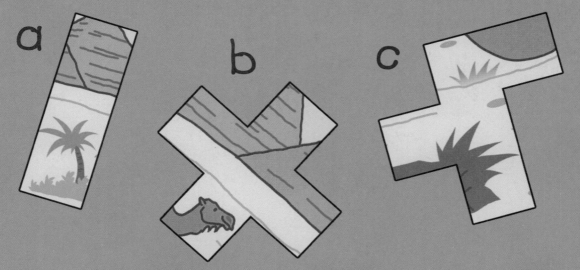

a

b

c

# Hidden picture

Look at this ice cream stand. Can you find the objects
pictured below? Check the boxes when you find them.

# Under the sea

Color in the underwater scene, using the colored dots as a guide.

# Who's missing?

Circle the bug that is in picture A but is missing from picture B.

# Jigsaw jumble

Which jigsaw piece completes the picture of Iguanodon?
Can you draw it in?

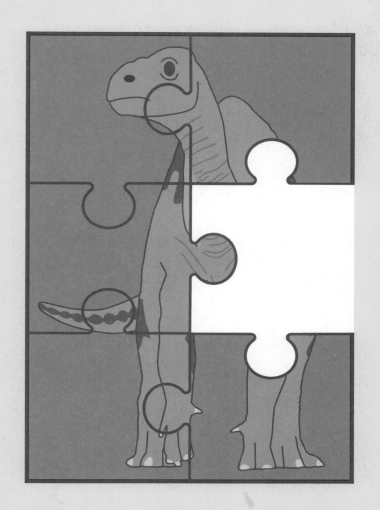

a

b

c

# Follow the trails

Baryonyx liked to eat fish. Follow the trails to find out which one leads to its favorite meal.

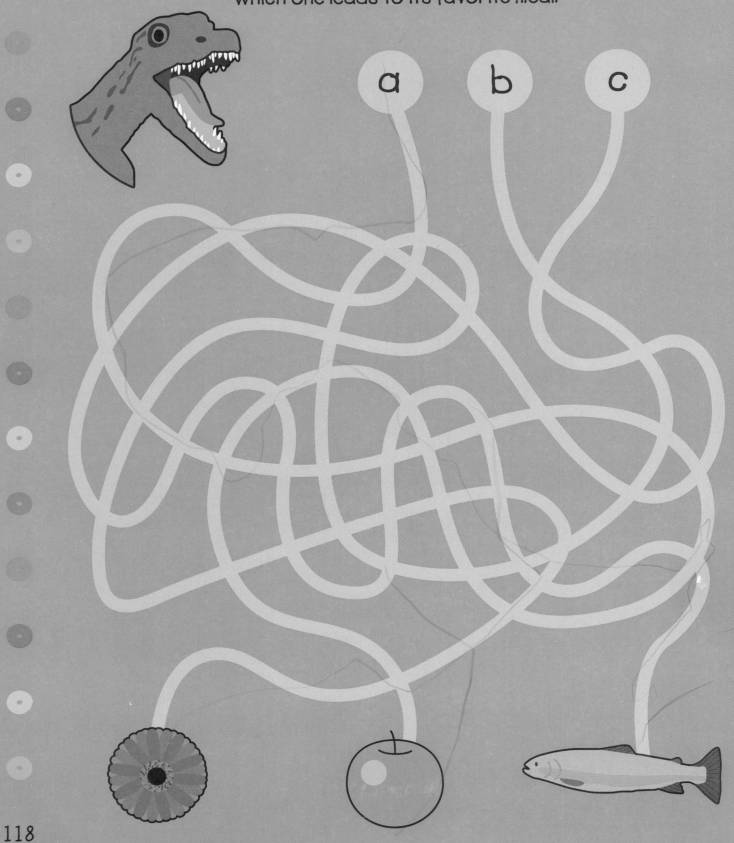

# Spot the difference

There are six differences between the two pictures of Triceratops.
Circle them when you find them.

## A

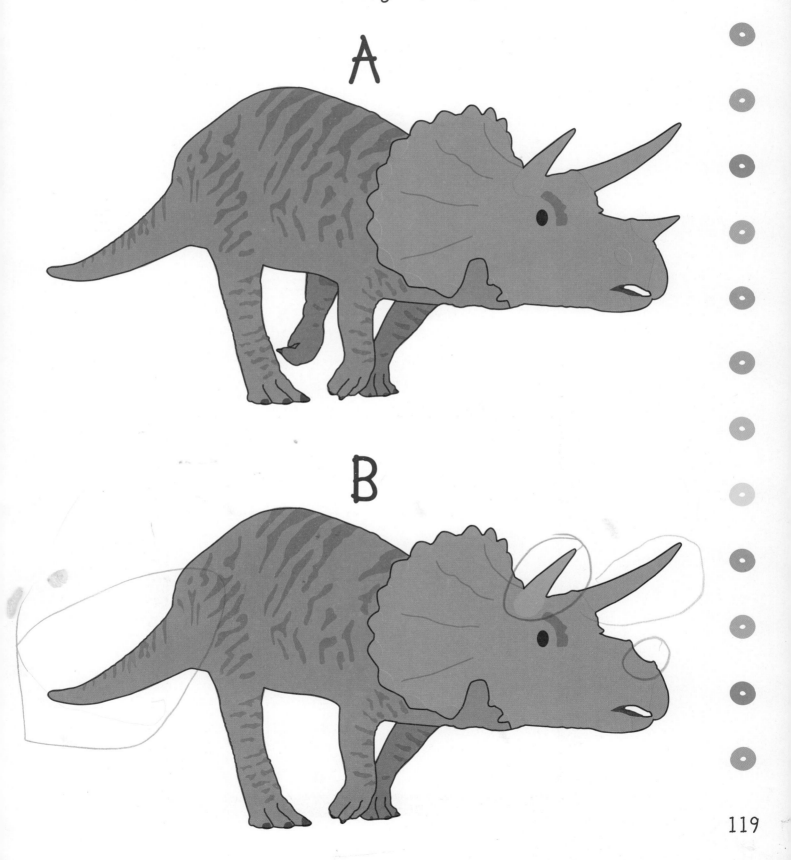

## B

# Number sudoku

Fill in the numbers 1, 2, 3, or 4 into the empty squares. Each number must appear once in each row, column, and box of four squares.

Look at the example:

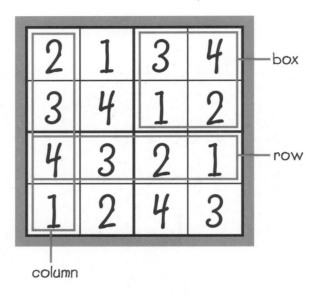

Now try these sudoku puzzles.

| | 3 | 1 | |
|---|---|---|---|
| 1 | | 3 | 4 |
| 2 | 1 | | 3 |
| | 4 | 2 | |

| 1 | | | 3 |
|---|---|---|---|
| 2 | 3 | | 4 |
| 3 | | 4 | |
| | 2 | 3 | |

# In the air

Circle three things that are wrong with this sky scene.

# First sounds

Draw a circle around the things that begin with the letter in the box.

# Match it

Draw a line between the foods on the plate and the words below.

sausages

cheese

bread

carrots

grapes

# Crossword

Use the picture clues to help you complete the seaside crossword.

1. sand castle

2. sea

3. beach

4. ice cream

5. bucket

3. b a

5. c

2. s

4. e

# Matching sports

Write over the names of the sports, and then draw lines
to match the words to the pictures.

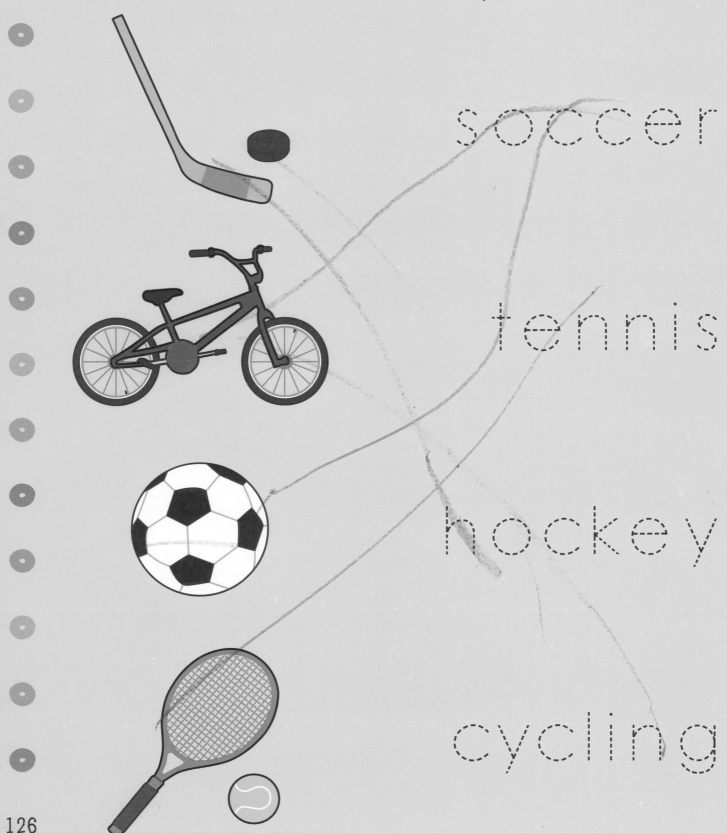

soccer

tennis

hockey

cycling

# Word search

Can you find the activities below in the word search?

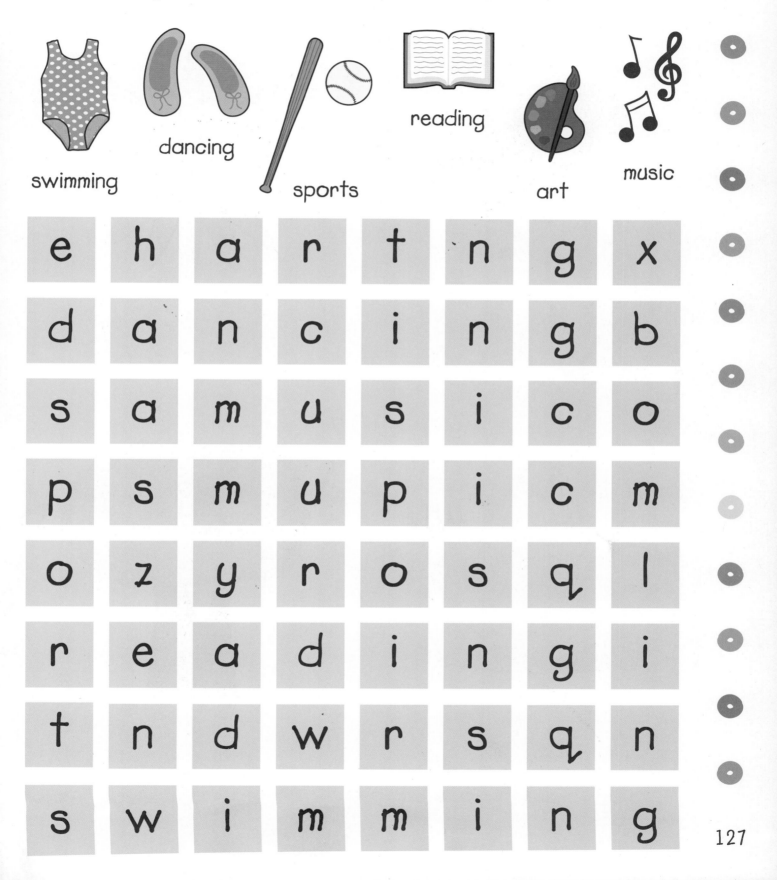

swimming

dancing

sports

reading

art

music

| e | h | a | r | t | n | g | x |
| d | a | n | c | i | n | g | b |
| s | a | m | u | s | i | c | o |
| p | s | m | u | p | i | c | m |
| o | z | y | r | o | s | q | l |
| r | e | a | d | i | n | g | i |
| t | n | d | w | r | s | q | n |
| s | w | i | m | m | i | n | g |

127

# In the yard

Write over the names of some things you might find in the yard.

bird    flower

pond    tree

# Hidden picture

Look at the station scene. Can you find the objects pictured below?
Check the boxes when you find them.

# Counting groups

Count each animal group and write the totals in the boxes below.
Can you also answer the questions?

## Jungle animals

Which animal doesn't have legs? Circle your answer.

## Under the sea

Which animal has claws? Circle your answer.

# Color match

Draw a line between the household objects
and the color word they match.

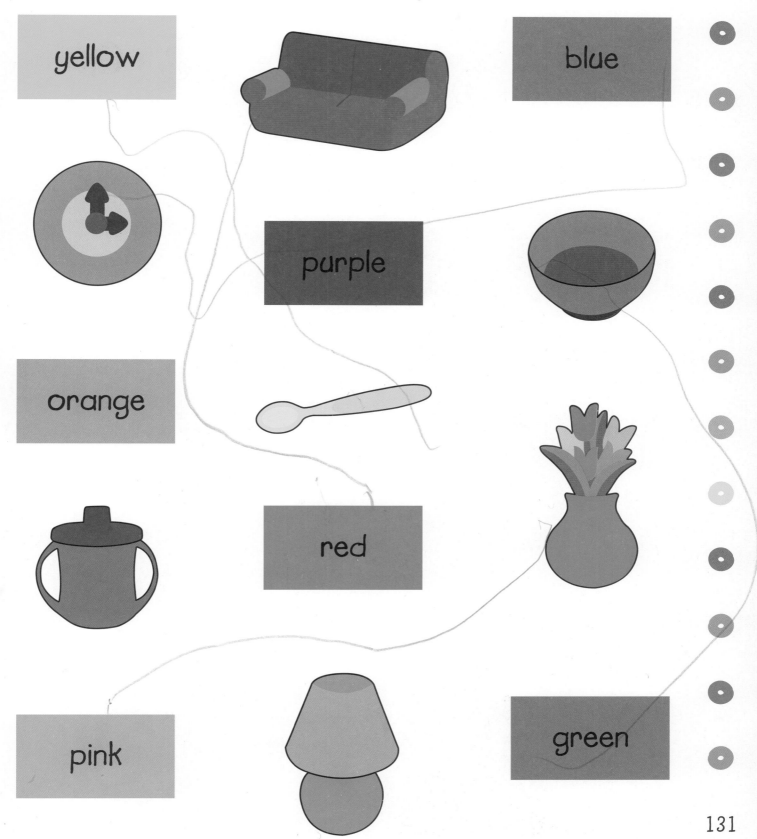

# Seek and find

The sea creatures below are all in the picture.
Check the boxes when you find them.

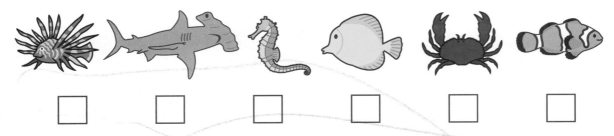

☐ ☐ ☐ ☐ ☐ ☐

# How to draw

Learn how to draw a duckling in three easy steps.

**1**

Draw a
half circle.

**2**

Draw a circle for
the head and
add a tail.

**3**

Give your duck
an eye, a beak,
and feet!

# How many?

Count the objects in each row, and then write the totals in the boxes.

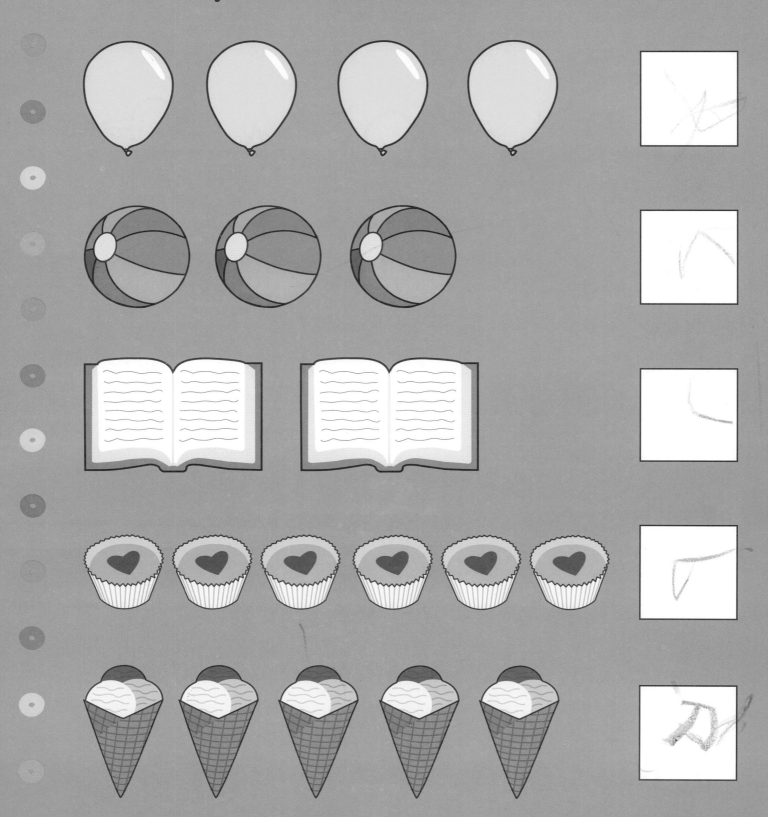

# Farm maze

Follow the green lines to find the quickest way through
the maze to get the tractor to the barn.

# Hidden picture

Look at this classroom. Can you find the objects pictured below?
Check the boxes when you find them.

# Machine math

Take the first group away from the second group,
and then write the totals in the boxes.

— means "take away"

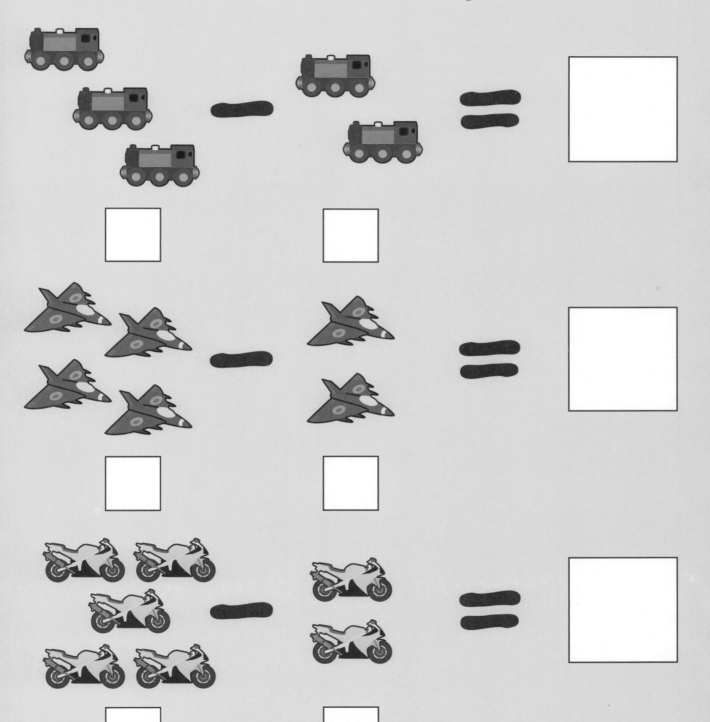

# Dot-to-dot

Connect the dots to draw the funny alien.
Color him in once your picture is complete.

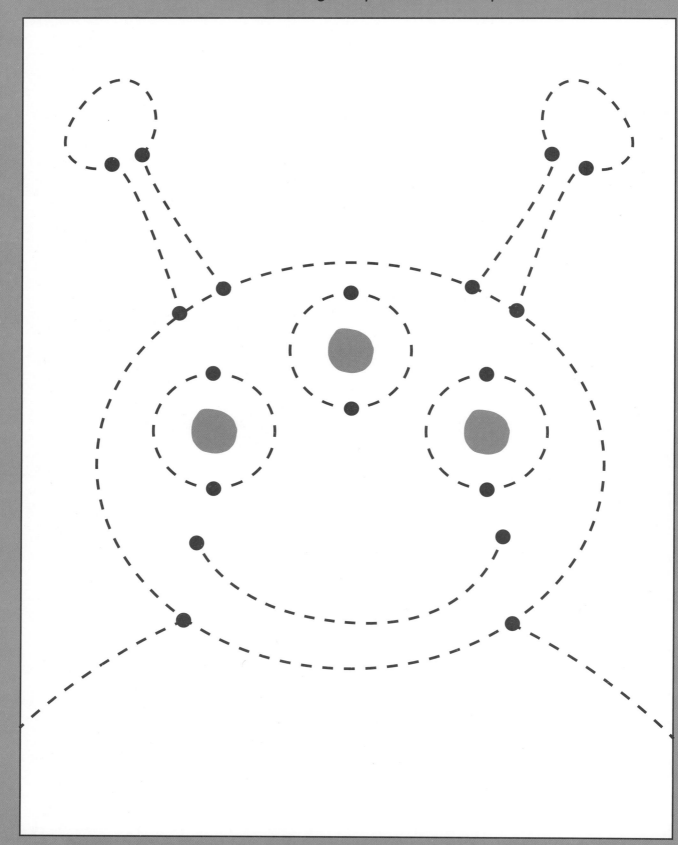

# Number questions

Count the numbers and write your answers in the boxes below.

8    5    9    7    3

7    9    8    9    8

8    7    9    5    8

How many number 5s?  ☐

How many number 7s?  ☐

How many number 9s?  ☐

How many number 8s?  ☐

How many number 3s?  ☐

# Find and count

Can you find and count the items below?
Check the boxes as you find them.

1 sand castle ☐

2 boats ☐

3 seagulls ☐

4 starfish ☐

5 palm trees ☐

6 crabs ☐

7 shells ☐

8 coconuts ☐

# Coloring fun

No one really knows for sure what color dinosaurs were,
so make this scene as colorful as you like.

# How to draw

Learn how to draw a palm tree in three easy steps.

**1**

Draw a square shape, like this.

**2**

Draw it three more times to make a trunk.

**3**

Finish by adding leaves to the top of the trunk.

# How to draw

Learn how to draw an erupting volcano in three easy steps.

**1**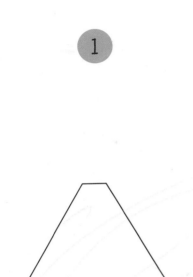

Draw a cone shape.

**2**

Draw smoke coming out of the volcano.

**3**

Finish by adding flames and hot lava.

143

# Matching numbers

Count each group of soccer things. Write over the numbers,
and then draw a line to the groups they match.

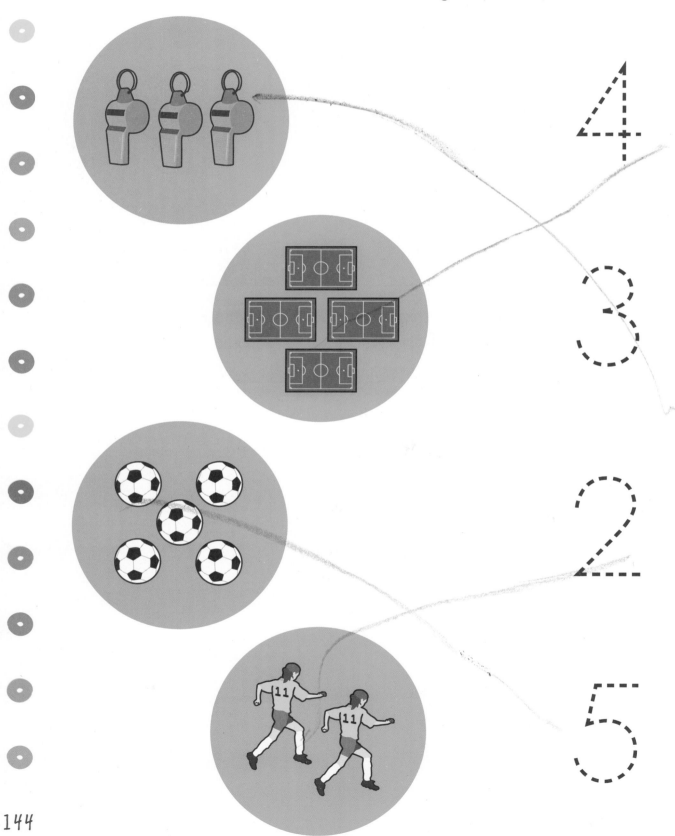

# Hide-and-seek

Look closely at the stable scene, and then answer
the counting questions.

How many
horseshoes
can you count?

How many
carrots can
you count?

How many
ponies are
in the field?

How many
yellow rosettes
are there?

# Missing halves

Can you draw the missing halves of these animal pictures?

 turtle

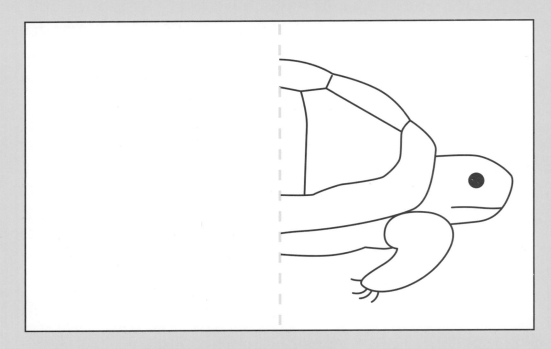

 tiger

# Toys galore

Count the toys, and then write your answers in the boxes.

teddy bears

toy cars

dolls

rubber ducks

toy trains

soccer balls

# Picture sequences

Color the last lollipop in each row to complete the patterns.

# Hidden picture

Look at this dragon's lair. Can you find the objects pictured below?
Check the boxes when you find them.

# Odd one out

Find the teddy bear that doesn't have a matching pair.

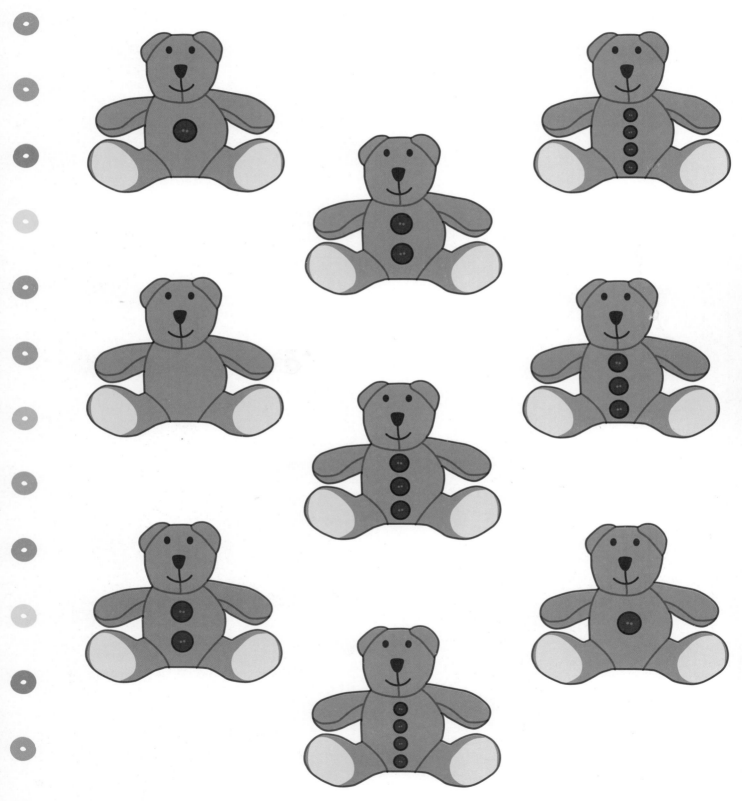

# Coloring fun

The rain forest is full of colorful animals. Find them and color them in.

# Job match

Draw a line to finish the sentences,
matching the person with their work vehicle.

concrete
mixer

I travel on
water in a . . .

I race to an
emergency in a . . .

cruise ship

I work on the
construction
site in a . . .

police
car

# Soccer maze

Follow the pink lines to find a way through the maze
to get the soccer player to the pitch.

# Hidden picture

Look at the castle scene. Can you find the objects pictured below?
Check the boxes when you find them.

# Spooky counting

Count and circle the objects below when you find them.

**five** shiny keys

**four** green toads

**three** blue potions

**two** hairy spiders

**one** wizard hat

# Color and create

Draw and color a pony show scene. Look at the pictures on the right for ideas, and add the things you like!

If Daisy jumps well, she will get a rosette.

Don't forget to draw Emily's riding helmet—why not make it really colorful?

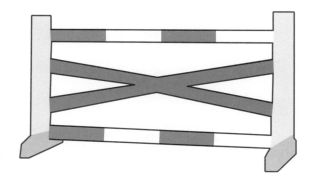

Why not draw a fence for Daisy to jump over at the show?

Ponies love to eat hay, so make sure Daisy has plenty to snack on.

Make sure Max the puppy doesn't get in the way!

You could also add some pretty flowers to the scene.

# Copy it

Can you draw a pirate hat? Draw it. Copy it. Color it in!

Look at the picture.                    Draw over the outline.

Now draw your own pirate hat and color it in.

# Copy it

Can you draw a cutlass? Draw it. Copy it. Color it in!

Look at the picture.                    Draw over the outline.

Now draw your own cutlass and color it in.

# Color me in

Color in this steam train using the colored dots as a guide.

# Spot the difference

There are six differences between the two pictures of a concrete mixer. Circle them when you find them.

## A

## B

# Hidden picture

Look at the picnic scene. Can you find the objects pictured below?
Check the boxes when you find them.

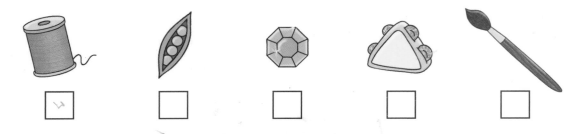

# Missing halves

Can you draw the missing halves of these animal pictures?

 butterfly

 panda

# Shape sudoku

Fill in the grids so that each shape appears once in each row, column, and box of four squares.

Look at the example:

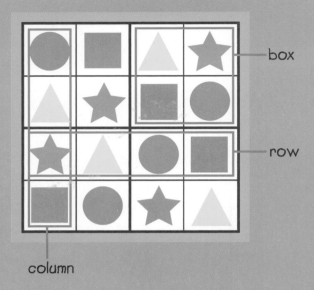

box

row

column

Now try these sudoku puzzles.

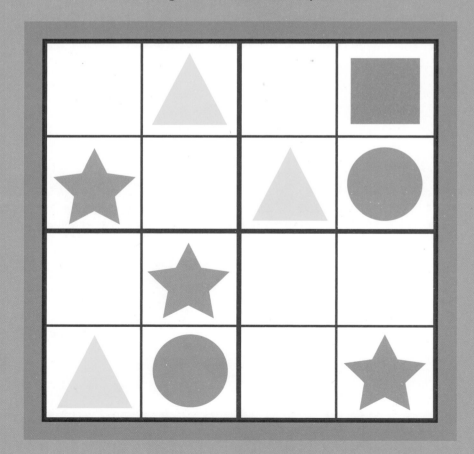

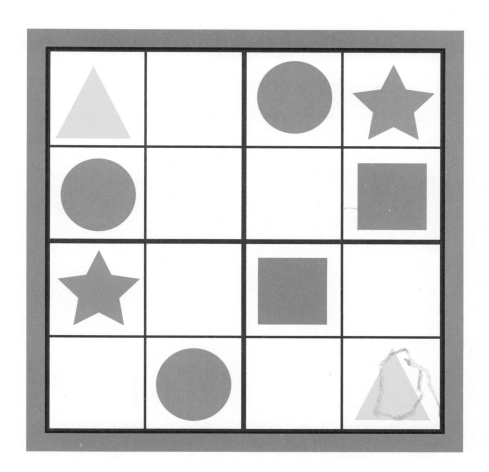

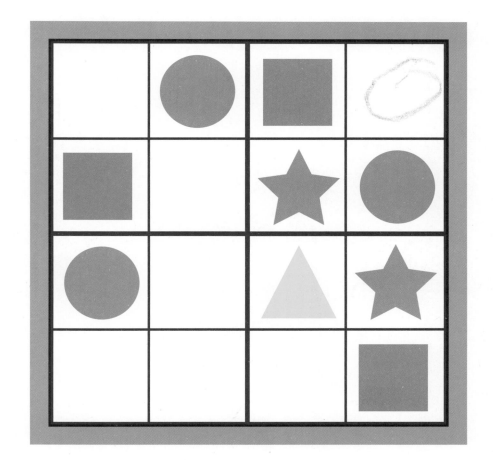

165

# Jigsaw jumble

Which jigsaw piece completes this treasure map?
Can you draw it in?

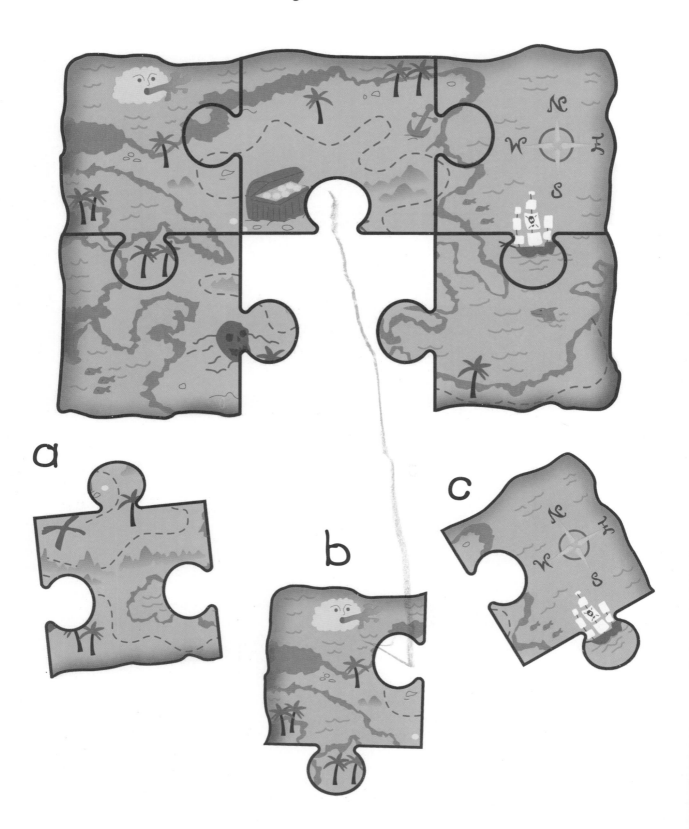

a

b

c

# Odd one out

Which of these objects would a pirate not use?

Which of these foods would you not feed to a horse?

# Spot the detail

Draw a line from the pictures to where they are on the jewelry box.

# Hidden picture

Look at the pet groomer's scene. Can you find the objects pictured below? Check the boxes when you find them.

# Picture sequences

Color the last fish in each row to complete the patterns.

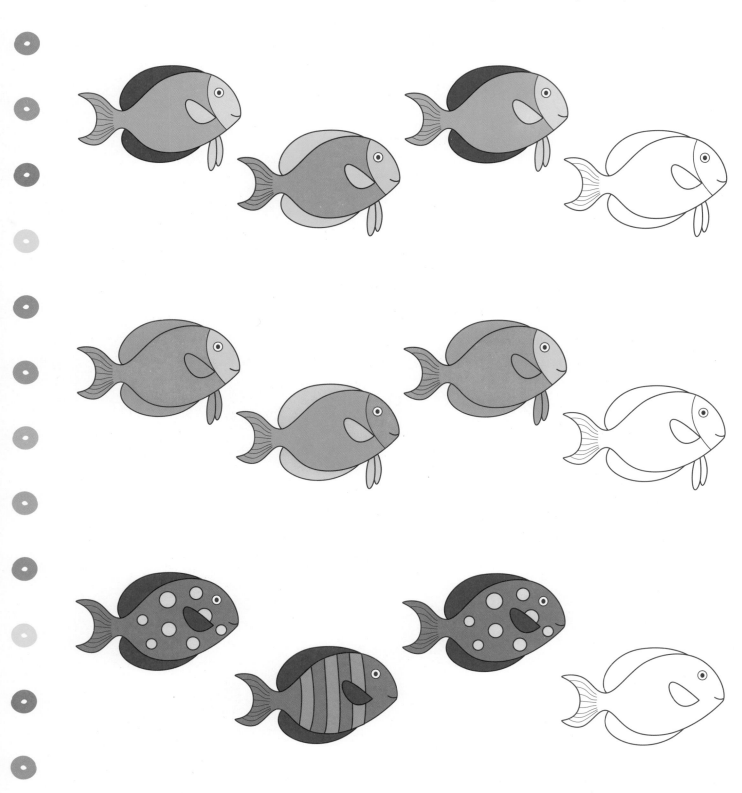

# Pony trails

Which trail leads Hannah and her pony to the winner's rosette?

# How to draw

Learn how to draw a rocket in three easy steps.

**1**

Draw the main rocket shape.

**2**

Draw the wings and the engine.

**3**

Give your rocket a large window and a cool design.

# Word puzzle

Use the word and picture clues to figure out what the four mixed-up words are. Write the letters in the correct spaces.

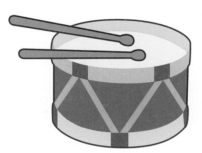

Makes lots of noise

Can fly very high

Has a pretty dress

Are very colorful

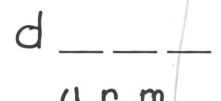

d _ _ _ _

u r m

k _ _ _

i e t

d _ _ _

l o l

p _ _ _ _ _

a t n i s

# I spy . . .

All of these things begin with one of the letters below, except one.
Circle it.

s     b     l     t

# Missing letters

Fill in the last letters of these different clothes words.

shoe __

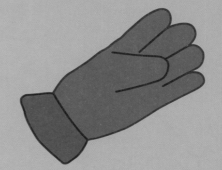

mitte __

T-shir __

ha __

ca __

dres __

# Word wheel

Fill in the missing letters of the words on the wheel. Then use these letters to spell the name of the vehicle at the bottom of the page.

_ractor

_ace car

_mbulance

f _ re truck

airpla _ e

_ _ _ _ _ _ _

# Crossword

Use the picture clues to help you complete the horsey crossword.

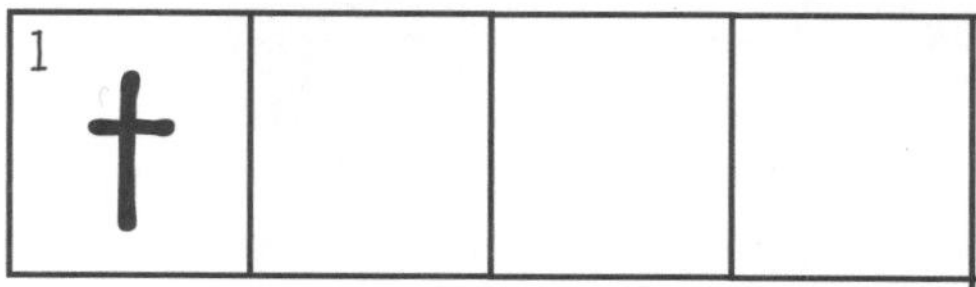

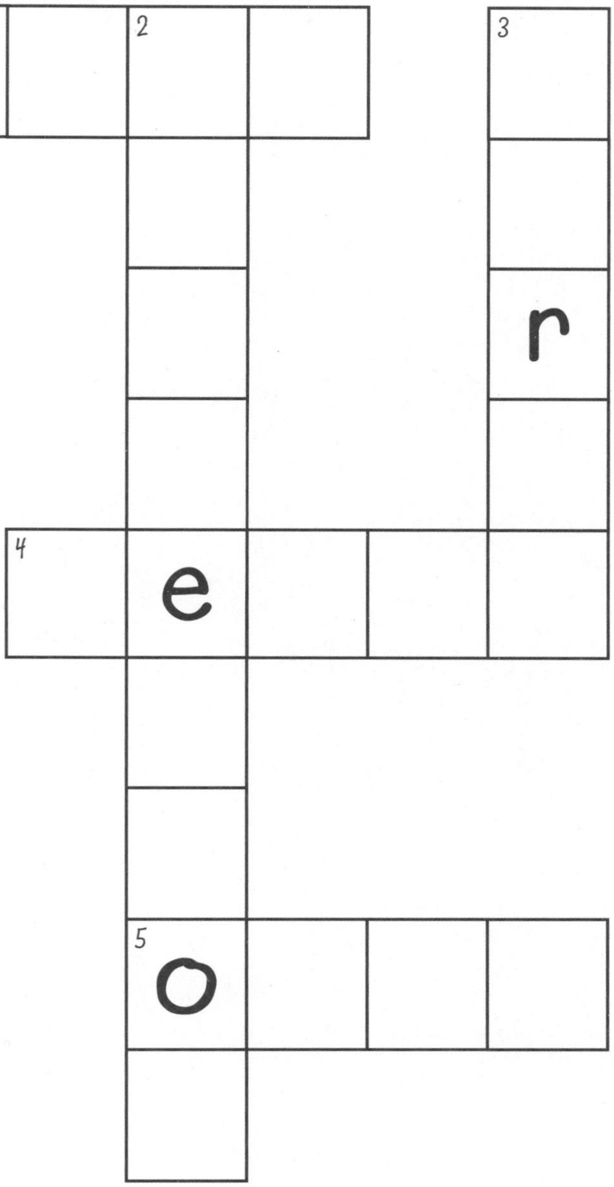


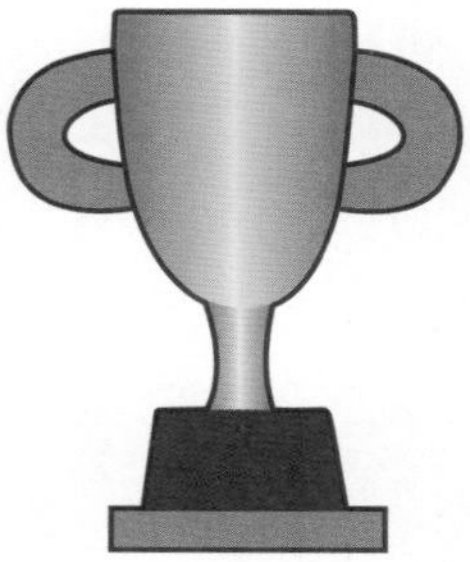

1. trophy

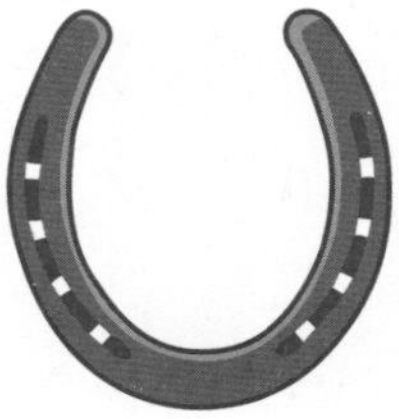

2. horseshoe

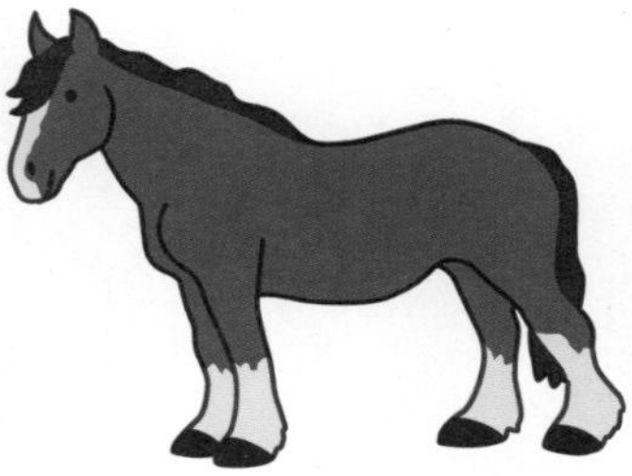

3. horse

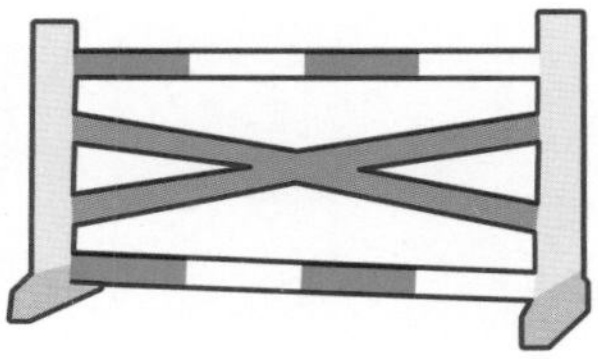

4. fence

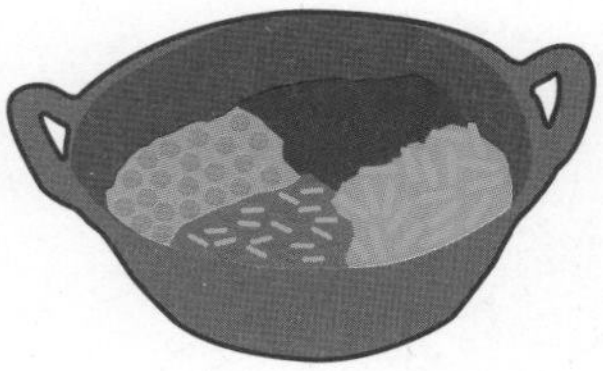

5. oats

# Hidden picture

Look at this toy store. Can you find the objects pictured below?
Check the boxes when you find them.

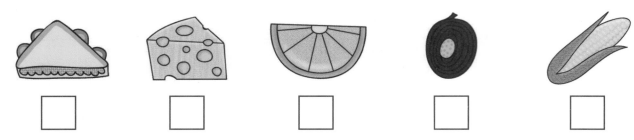

# Colorful flags

Color in the big flags using the little flags as a color guide.

Canada

Seychelles

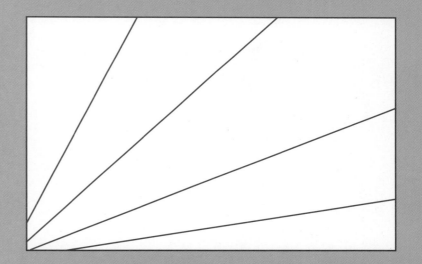

Kenya

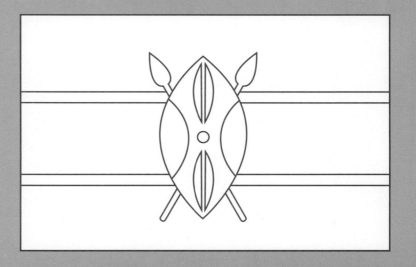

# Matching rhymes

Draw lines between each of the rhyming pairs.

cat

frog

map

pen

man

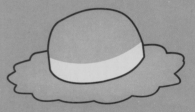

hat

hen

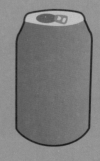

can

dog

cap

# Missing letters

Complete the dinosaur sentences by filling in the missing letters.
The pictures will help you.

Triceratops has three pointed

h __ __ __ __

On its feet, Iguanodon
has two big

c __ __ __ __

Stegosaurus's tail has sharp

s __ __ __ __ __ __

Baryonyx has very sharp

t __ __ __ __

# Word search

Can you find the pirate words in the word search?

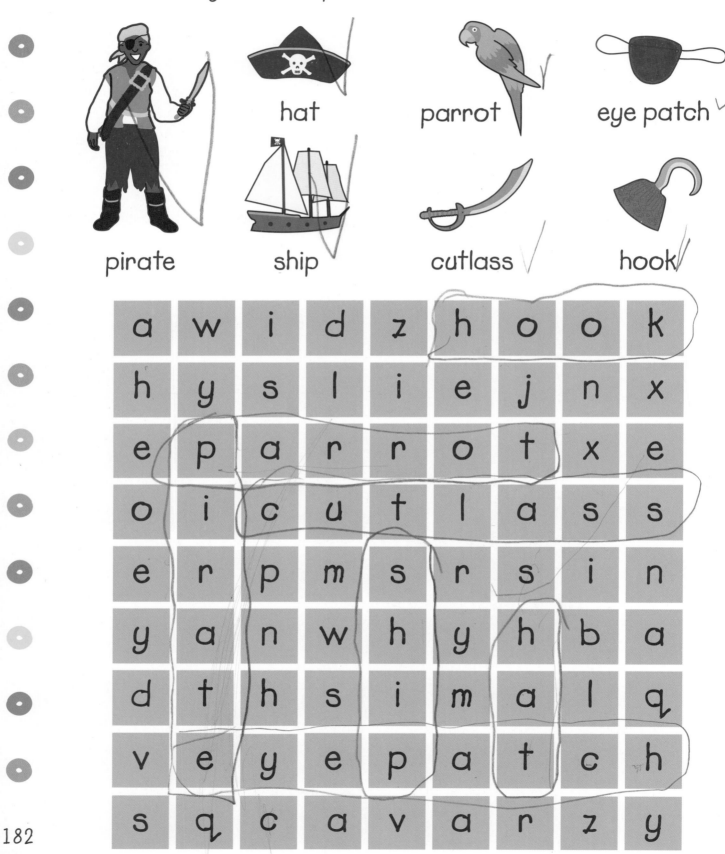

hat

parrot

eye patch

pirate

ship

cutlass

hook

| a | w | i | d | z | h | o | o | k |
|---|---|---|---|---|---|---|---|---|
| h | y | s | l | i | e | j | n | x |
| e | p | a | r | r | o | t | x | e |
| o | i | c | u | t | l | a | s | s |
| e | r | p | m | s | r | s | i | n |
| y | a | n | w | h | y | h | b | a |
| d | t | h | s | i | m | a | l | q |
| v | e | y | e | p | a | t | c | h |
| s | q | c | a | v | a | r | z | y |

# Princess puzzle

Can you draw lines to match each princess accessory to its first letter?

j

d

w

m

h

t

c

# Halving numbers

When you halve a number, the amount you take away is the same as the number left over. Follow the instructions below to find the answers.

Cross out one teddy bear to make **half of 2.**

  =

Cross out two dolls to make **half of 4.**

     =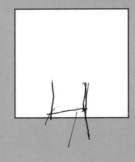

Cross out three ducks to make **half of 6.**

  =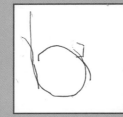

Cross out four toy soldiers to make **half of 8.**

  =

# How many?

Count the objects in each row, and then write the totals in the boxes.

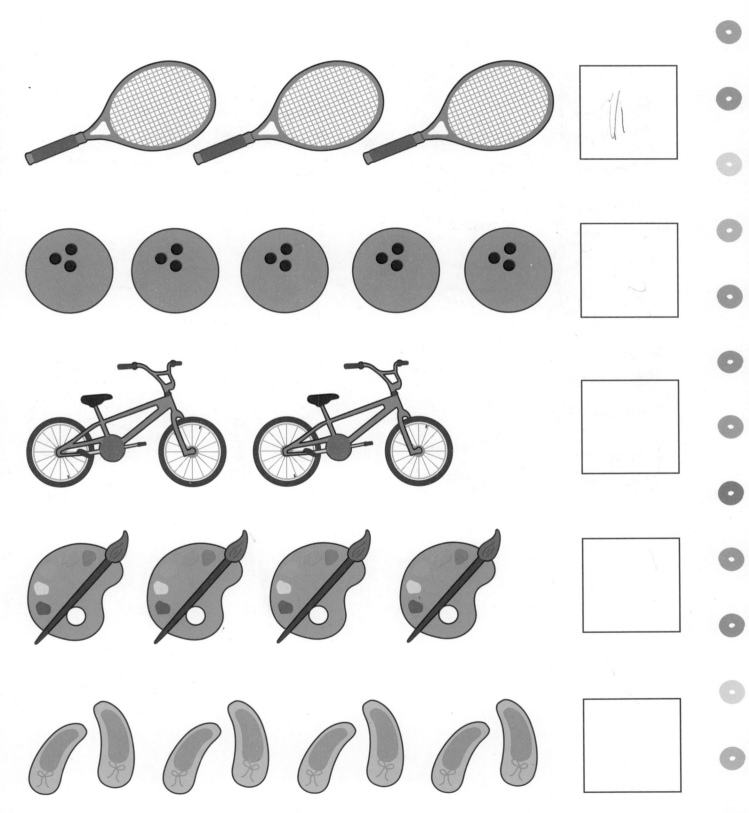

# Hide-and-seek

Look closely at the pirate scene,
and then answer the counting questions below.

How many
parrots
can you count?

How many
eye patches
can you count?

How many
pirate hats can
you count?

How many
pirates are
holding
cutlasses?

# Dot-to-dot

Connect the dots to finish this train picture, and then color it in.

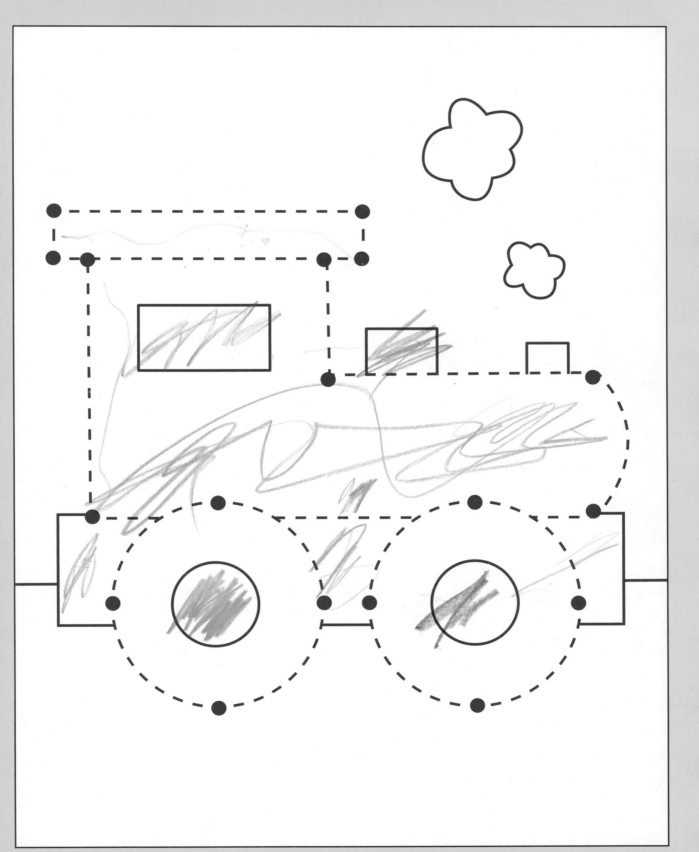

# How old am I?

How old is Smokey the dragon?
Count the candles on each cake and write your answers in the boxes.

# Hidden picture

Look at this sky scene. Can you find the objects pictured below?
Check the boxes when you find them.

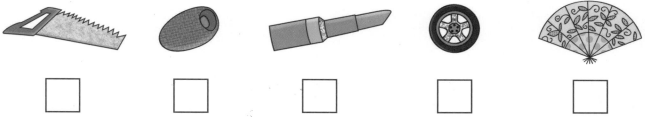

# Number sudoku

Fill in the numbers 1, 2, 3, or 4 into the empty squares. Each number must appear once in each row, column, and box of four squares.

Look at the example:

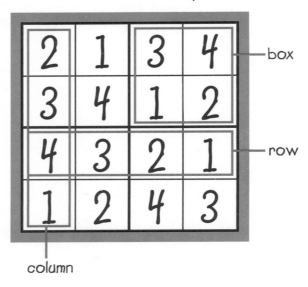

box

row

column

Now try these sudoku puzzles.

|   | 4 |   | 3 |
|---|---|---|---|
| 3 | 2 |   | 1 |
| 4 |   | 1 |   |
|   | 1 |   | 4 |

| 1 |   | 4 | 2 |
|---|---|---|---|
| 2 |   |   | 1 |
|   |   | 2 |   |
| 3 | 2 |   | 4 |

| | 1 | 3 | 4 |
|---|---|---|---|
| 3 |   |   |   |
|   | 3 | 2 | 1 |
| 1 |   |   | 3 |

# Answers

## Page 2

## Page 3

## Page 5

## Page 6

5 is the odd one out

## Page 7

## Page 9

rose, leaf, snail, sun

## Page 12

c

## Page 15

## Page 17

Japan/Sushi,  Italy/Pizza,  United Kingdom/Fish and chips

## Page 18

## Page 19

## Page 21

| g | t | r | a | c | t | o | r |   |
|---|---|---|---|---|---|---|---|---|
| c | f | a | k | q | g | e |   | p |
| a | o | m | i | f | x | l |   | i |
| l | s | c | d | l | t | a |   | g |
| f | o | a | l | y | s | m |   | s |
| k | r | l | o | a | l | b | e |
| u | s | f | a | r | m | e | r |

**Page 22**

**Page 24**

Trees: d, a, c, b.          Sandwiches: a, d, b, c

**Page 25**

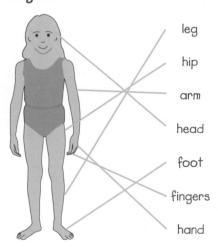

**Page 26**

leg

hip

arm

head

foot

fingers

hand

**Page 28**

square, triangle, heart, circle
The letters make the word: star

**Page 29**

yellow   green   purple   red

blue   orange   pink

**Page 30**

blue  orange

pink   red

green   yellow

**Pages 32–33**

| 4 | 2 | 3 | 1 |
|---|---|---|---|
| 3 | 1 | 2 | 4 |
| 1 | 3 | 4 | 2 |
| 2 | 4 | 1 | 3 |

| 1 | 4 | 3 | 2 |
|---|---|---|---|
| 3 | 2 | 1 | 4 |
| 4 | 1 | 2 | 3 |
| 2 | 3 | 4 | 1 |

| 4 | 1 | 2 | 3 |
|---|---|---|---|
| 3 | 2 | 4 | 1 |
| 1 | 4 | 3 | 2 |
| 2 | 3 | 1 | 4 |

**Page 34**

**Page 37**

**Page 39**

## Pages 40–41

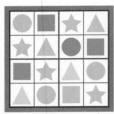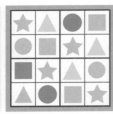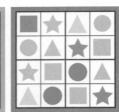

## Page 43

```
    ¹g
²l i o n
    r
    a        ⁵e        ⁴p
    f        l         a
    f        e         n
⁶l e o p a r d         a
             h         a
             a
             ³m o n k e y
             t
```

## Page 45

## Page 46
b

## Page 48

## Page 49
c is for cat, d is for dog, f is for fish,
k is for kitten, m is for mouse, p is for puppy,
r is for rabbit, t is for turtle

## Page 51

6          3          5          4

## Page 53
7 goldfish, 2 rabbits, 6 guinea pigs, 3 puppies,
4 turtles, 5 mice

## Page 56

baa baa           cock-a-doodle-doo

quack           moo

oink           naa naa

## Page 57

## Page 58

rectangle     circle     square     star     triangle

## Pages 60–61

| 2 | 3 | 1 | 4 |
|---|---|---|---|
| 1 | 4 | 2 | 3 |
| 3 | 1 | 4 | 2 |
| 4 | 2 | 3 | 1 |

| 4 | 1 | 3 | 2 |
|---|---|---|---|
| 2 | 3 | 1 | 4 |
| 3 | 4 | 2 | 1 |
| 1 | 2 | 4 | 3 |

| 3 | 1 | 4 | 2 |
|---|---|---|---|
| 2 | 4 | 3 | 1 |
| 4 | 2 | 1 | 3 |
| 1 | 3 | 2 | 4 |

## Page 62
c

## Page 63
c

## Page 64

## Page 66

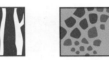

## Page 68

tiger     zebra     giraffe     leopard

## Page 70

## Page 71

## Page 72

## Page 73
c

## Page 74
3, 4, 2

## Page 75

frog     tiger     gorilla     snake     toucan

## Page 76

## Page 77
camel, zebra, whale, emu

## Page 78
Underwater animals: c, b, d, a    Wild animals: b, c, d, a

## Page 81

4     5     3     8     8 legs

## Page 82

## Page 84

## Page 85
10 stars, 5 arms, 3 horns

## Page 86
chair, duck, book, ball

195

## Page 87

## Page 89

4, 8, 3, 8 (double 4), 4

## Page 92

## Page 93

## Page 94

2 + 1 = 3     2 + 2 = 4     4 + 4 = 8

## Page 95

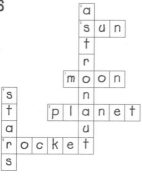   4 zebras

## Page 96

## Page 97

## Pages 98-99

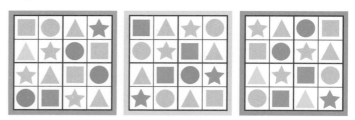

## Page 100

## Page 101

## Page 102

## Page 104

3 rockets, 7 moons, 2 space shuttles, 6 astronauts, 4 planets, 5 suns

196

## Page 107

## Pages 108-109

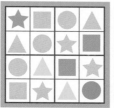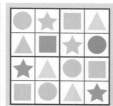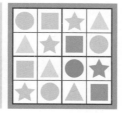

## Page 111

There is no bus.

## Page 112

Australia    France    Chile    United States of America

## Page 113
b

## Page 114

## Page 116

## Page 118
c

## Page 119

## Pages 120-121

## Page 122

## Page 123

## Page 124

grapes    sausages    carrots    bread    cheese

## Page 125

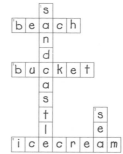

## Page 126

hockey

cycling

soccer

tennis

## Page 127

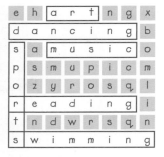

## Page 129

## Page 130
4 jungle animals
6 underwater animals

## Page 131

| red | blue | green | purple | yellow | pink | orange |

## Page 132

## Page 134
4, 3, 2, 6, 5

## Page 135

## Page 136

## Page 137
3 − 2 = 1          4 − 2 = 2          5 − 2 = 3

## Page 139
2, 3, 4, 5, 1

## Page 144

3          4          5          2

## Page 145
7, 10, 2, 4

## Page 147
3 teddy bears, 5 toy cars, 6 dolls, 2 rubber ducks,
4 toy trains, 5 soccer balls

## Page 148

198

**Page 149**

**Page 150**

**Page 152**

cruise ship    police car    concrete mixer

**Page 153**

**Page 154**

**Page 161**

**Page 162**

**Page 164–165**

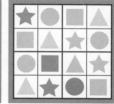

**Page 166**

a

**Page 167**

**Page 168**

**Page 169**

**Page 170**

199

## Page 171
a

## Page 173
drum, kite, doll, paints

## Page 174
doll

## Page 175
shoes, mitten, T-shirt, hat, cap, dress

## Page 176
tractor, race car, ambulance, fire truck, airplane
The letters make the word: train

## Page 177

| | t | r | o | p | h | y | | | h | |
| | | | | | o | | | | o | |
| | | | | | r | | | | r | |
| | | | | | s | | | | s | |
| | | f | e | n | c | e | | | e | |
| | | | | | s | | | | | |
| | | | | | h | | | | | |
| | | o | a | t | s | | | | | |
| | | | | | e | | | | | |

## Page 178

## Page 180
cat/hat, map/cap, man/can, hen/pen, dog/frog

## Page 181
horns, claws, spikes, teeth

## Page 182

| a | w | i | d | z | h | o | o | k |
| h | y | s | l | i | e | j | n | x |
| e | p | a | r | r | o | t | x | e |
| o | i | c | u | t | l | a | s | s |
| e | r | p | m | s | r | s | i | n |
| y | a | n | w | h | y | h | b | a |
| d | t | h | s | i | m | a | l | q |
| v | e | y | e | p | a | t | c | h |
| s | q | c | a | v | a | r | z | y |

## Page 183
c is for castle, d is for dress, h is for hat,
j is for jewels, m is for mirror, t is for tiara,
w is for wand,

## Page 184
1, 2, 3, 4

## Page 185
3, 5, 2, 4, 8

## Page 186
5, 8, 6, 2

## Page 188
5, 8, 6

## Page 189

## Pages 190–191

| 1 | 4 | 2 | 3 |
| 3 | 2 | 4 | 1 |
| 4 | 3 | 1 | 2 |
| 2 | 1 | 3 | 4 |

| 1 | 3 | 4 | 2 |
| 2 | 4 | 3 | 1 |
| 4 | 1 | 2 | 3 |
| 3 | 2 | 1 | 4 |

| 2 | 1 | 3 | 4 |
| 3 | 4 | 1 | 2 |
| 4 | 3 | 2 | 1 |
| 1 | 2 | 4 | 3 |